CONTEMPO

English Connections
GRAMMAR FOR COMMUNICATION
BOOK 3

CATHERINE PORTER

ELIZABETH MINICZ

Project Editor
Michael O'Neill

CONTEMPORARY BOOKS
a division of NTC/CONTEMPORARY PUBLISHING GROUP
Lincolnwood, Illinois USA

Library of Congress Cataloging-in-Publication Data

Porter, Catherine.
   English connections. Book 3 : grammar for communication / Catherine Porter & Elizabeth Minicz.
      p.   cm.
   ISBN 0-8092-4207-9
      1. English language—Textbooks for foreign speakers. 2. English language—Grammar—Problems, exercises,
   etc. 3. Communication—Problems, exercises, etc. I. Minicz, Elizabeth. II. Title.
   PE1128.P587 1994
   428.2′4—dc20   94-20479
                                                                  CIP

ISBN: 0-8092-4207-9

Published by Contemporary Books,
a division of NTC/Contemporary Publishing Group, Inc.,
4255 West Touhy Avenue,
Lincolnwood (Chicago), Illinois 60646-1975 U.S.A.
© 1994 by Catherine Porter and Elizabeth Minicz
All rights reserved. No part of this book may be reproduced,
stored in a retrieval system, or transmitted in any form or by any means,
electronic, mechanical, photocopying, recording, or otherwise,
without prior permission of the publisher.
Manufactured in the United States of America.

8 9 0 GB(H)) 10 9 8 7 6 5

Editorial Director
Mark Boone

Editorial
Craig Bolt
Kathleen Ossip
Lisa Black
Lisa Dillman
Ann Wambach

Editorial Production Manager
Norma Underwood

Production Editor
Thomas D. Scharf

Cover Design
Georgene Sainati

Illustrator
David Will

Line Art
William Colrus
Jeff Weyer

Art & Production
Jan Geist
Sue Springston

Typography
Ellen Kollmon

Cover Photograph
© Westlight

Special thanks to
Caren Van Slyke

Contents

Introduction v

Unit 1: Who's that? 1
Simple Present ♦ Vocabulary: Time Expressions ♦ Simple Present—Stative Verbs ♦ Simple Present vs. Present Continuous ♦ Meanings of *Have*

Unit 2: I used to work for a magazine 11
Simple Past of Regular and Irregular Verbs ♦ *Used to* ♦ *Used to: Wh*-Questions ♦ Vocabulary: Adjectives That Describe Feelings ♦ *Not . . . anymore* ♦ *But* ♦ *Didn't use to*

Unit 3: Have you ever changed a tire? 21
Past Participles: Regular and Irregular ♦ Pronunciation of Past Participles ♦ Present Perfect ♦ Present Perfect with *Never* and *Always* ♦ Vocabulary: Sports

Review: Units 1-3 31

Unit 4: How long have you lived here? 33
Present Perfect with Time Expressions ♦ Vocabulary: Time Expressions with *For* and *Since* ♦ Present Perfect vs. Simple Past

Unit 5: Would you pick that up, please? 43
Commands and Requests ♦ Two-Word Verbs ♦ Vocabulary: More Two-Word Verbs ♦ Two-Word Verbs (Separable and Inseparable) ♦ Two-Word Verbs with Pronouns

Unit 6: I'd like a cup of decaf, please 53
Polite Offers and Requests with *Would like* ♦ *Would rather/Would rather not* ♦ Vocabulary: Different Kinds of Clothing ♦ *One/Ones/Another one* ♦ Review of Singular and Plural Nouns

Review: Units 4-6 63

Unit 7: I'm going to make eggplant curry 65
Noncount Nouns ♦ Vocabulary: Quantifiers for Noncount Nouns ♦ Nouns with No Article ♦ Future with *Going to*

Unit 8: We gave her a big cake 75
Direct and Indirect Objects ♦ Indirect Object Pronouns ♦ Verbs with *To* and *For* ♦ Vocabulary: Household Objects ♦ *Too* + Adjective ♦ *So* and *Because*

Unit 9: I've got to find a job fast 85
Modals of Necessity ♦ *Would like* + Infinitive ♦ Present Perfect Continuous ♦ Vocabulary: Reduced Forms

Review: Units 7-9 95

Unit 10: I'm glad I ran into you 97
Commands with *You* ♦ Vocabulary: Prepositions of Movement
♦ Vocabulary: Discount Stores ♦ Inseparable Two-Word Verbs

Unit 11: Who's the oldest person alive? 107
Modals of Probability ♦ Reflexive Pronouns ♦ Other Uses of
Reflexive Pronouns ♦ Superlatives

Unit 12: Which one is more expensive? 117
Present Perfect Simple and Continuous ♦ Review of Comparatives
and Superlatives ♦ Comparisons with *As* + Adjective + *As*
♦ Vocabulary: Descriptive Comparisons

Review: Units 10-12 127

Unit 13: I was walking down Park Street when it happened 129
Past Continuous ♦ Past Continuous: Questions and Negative
Statements ♦ Vocabulary: Phrases for Describing People
♦ Simple Past/Past Continuous with *When* ♦ Simple Past/Past
Continuous with *While*

Unit 14: What a surprise! 139
Relative Clauses with *Who* ♦ Vocabulary: Jobs ♦ Relative Clauses
with *Which* and *That* ♦ Relative Clauses: Word Order

Unit 15: I'll miss you all! 149
Future with *Will* and *Won't* ♦ Future Conditional ♦ Vocabulary:
Weather Conditions ♦ Factual Conditional ♦ Reflexive Pronouns/
Each other

Review: Units 13-15 159

Teacher Script for Listening Exercises 161

Appendix 164

Answer Key 178

Acknowledgments

Diane Larsen-Freeman
Chief Consultant
Master of Arts in Teaching (MAT) Program
School for International Training, Brattleboro, Vermont

Judy Hanlon, Oxnard Adult School, Oxnard, California

Renee Klosz, Lindsey Hopkins Technical Education Center, Miami, Florida

Suzanne Leibman, College of Lake County, Grayslake, Illinois

Fatiha Makloufi, Community Development Agency, New York, New York

Sharon O'Malley, Region IV Educational Service Center, Houston, Texas

Catherine Porter, Adult Education Service Center, Des Plaines, Illinois

Betsy Rubin, Chicago, Illinois

Darcy Jack, Pueblo High School, Tucson, Arizona

Aida Walqui, Stanford University, Stanford, California

Introduction

English Connections: Grammar for Communication is a three-level series for beginning to low-intermediate adult learners of English as a second language. It integrates a developmental grammar syllabus with real-life contexts within the framework of the communicative approach to language teaching.

The goal of this series is to help language learners use grammar accurately, meaningfully, and appropriately so that they can communicate effectively outside the classroom.

The inspiration behind *English Connections* is Diane Larsen-Freeman's framework for teaching grammar. It focuses on the three dimensions of grammar: form, meaning, and use. All three dimensions are equally important. Throughout this series, information on form, meaning, and use is presented whenever appropriate.

Grammar points that naturally occur together are presented and practiced within meaningful contexts through activities that are student-centered and highly interactive. Useful vocabulary relating to the contexts is also integrated into the lessons. The purpose of this series is to encourage grammatical accuracy within useful contexts that promote real communication in English. This is grammar for communication.

The Form / Meaning / Use Framework of *English Connections*

This series goes beyond a focus on form to include the dimensions of meaning and use as well. What do we mean by these terms? Let's look at an example from Book 3. Reflexive pronouns (*myself, yourself, herself, himself, itself, ourselves, yourselves, themselves*) are introduced in Unit 11.

How are reflexive pronouns formed?

The form of reflexive pronouns is described visually in a paradigm in the grammar box on page 111. Note that reflexive pronouns are the only pronouns in English with a form distinction between the second-person singular and the second-person plural (*yourself—yourselves*).

What do reflexive pronouns mean?

Reflexive pronouns are grouped together in appropriate contexts in Unit 11 to help clarify their meaning. These pronouns indicate that the direct or indirect recipient of an action is the same as the agent of that action. (*Sergio hurt himself. Tan is teaching himself to play the guitar.*) In combination with certain verbs or prepositions, reflexive pronouns can have other special meanings as well (*Dora did the job by herself = Dora did the job without help*).

When are reflexive pronouns used?

Reflexive pronouns are usually used when the action by a subject or agent is performed upon itself. However, they are usually not used for actions performed by an agent upon parts of that agent's body. (*I wash my hands.* NOT **I wash myself the hands.*) This usage may differ from that of students' native languages. Compare the Spanish *Me lavo las manos*, for example. English reflexive pronouns can also be used for emphasis. (*I myself would do that differently.*)

From this example we can see that teaching a grammar point involves teaching not only the form but the meaning and use as well. Information on form, meaning, and use for each grammar point is provided in detail in *English Connections, Book 3 Teacher's Edition*, especially in the Grammar Guide page that precedes the step-by-step teaching suggestions for each unit.

Learning a Second Language

People learn a second language in many different ways. For example, visual learners learn best by looking at graphic representations of concepts. Auditory learners learn best by listening to explanations. Kinesthetic/tactile learners learn best by manipulating objects and moving around.

English Connections addresses a variety of learning styles. For example, graphic icons represent directions to visual learners, and there are grammar boxes designed to aid these learners as well. Listening exercises along with pair and small-group activities encourage auditory learners. Total Physical Response (TPR) activities appeal to kinesthetic/tactile learners.

Language learning is a gradual process, and people learn about form, meaning, and use little by little. In *English Connections*, only one part of a grammar point is presented at a time. More information about form, meaning, and use unfolds as learners gain familiarity with grammar points, which are recycled for continuous practice. Finally, review units provide practice in freer, less-structured real-life contexts.

About the Series

English Connections: Grammar for Communication consists of:

- Three student books
- Three teacher's editions
- Three workbooks
- Two audiocassettes for each level of the series

Each student book has fifteen units, five review units, a teacher script for listening exercises, an appendix with mini-exercises, and an answer key.

Each teacher's edition includes a detailed scope-and-sequence chart and full-page representations from the student book with cues for the workbook. Each unit contains a Grammar Guide page with useful background information about each grammar point, step-by-step teaching suggestions, extension activities, and a complete answer key.

Each workbook provides extended focused practice for grammar and vocabulary from each unit in the student book.

The audiocassettes include all listening exercises (also in the teacher script), all dialogues other than writing exercises, and most of the Connections and Small Talk sections.

Teaching *English Connections*

Gray bars are used in each unit to signal a logical stopping point in the text. This feature can be useful in planning classroom time, since you will not be able to complete an entire unit in one class period.

All four language skills (Listening, Speaking, Reading, and Writing) are integrated from the very beginning in Unit One. To identify the language skills that are practiced in each exercise, graphic symbols are used as pre-reading cues. Many times they are used in combination, since more than one skill is practiced at a time.

The following notes describe the recurring features in the student book.

Opening Illustrations

Each unit opens with an illustration that provides a natural setting for the grammar points and vocabulary of the unit.

Elicit from students as much language as you can about the picture. Ask questions about the people and encourage students to guess what is happening.

Setting the Scene

This regular feature consists of a short conversation using authentic language that provides a context for the grammar points of the unit.

Introduce the characters in the conversation. Then read the conversation aloud a few times as naturally as possible. Have students practice it in pairs and listen to them practice.

Don't correct every mistake you hear—this may make students hesitate to speak. Instead, write down one or two common mistakes that you may hear. Then tell the class as a group to repeat the correct pronunciation after you and encourage accuracy on those points.

Grammar Boxes

The grammar boxes include many examples, and students are encouraged to guess the rule.

Choose examples from the box and write them on the board. Elicit more examples from the students. After giving many examples, elicit the rule from the students or, if necessary, present it in your own words. After presenting the grammar point orally, use the grammar box as a summary of the form/meaning/use information. (The teacher's editions provide step-by-step teaching suggestions for each grammar point.)

The presentation of each grammar point is followed by a combination of focused and communicative practice. The goal is to help students learn to use the grammar for communication.

Focus on Vocabulary

To develop a meaningful context, relevant vocabulary is introduced. Vocabulary boxes are interspersed throughout each unit as needed.

Bring in realia (real objects) or draw pictures on the board to illustrate words. Ask questions using the words in the box.

Connections

This feature occurs as the need arises. It helps students develop strategies for communicating in a second language and is followed by activities that allow students to practice the strategy.

Model the strategy with a more advanced student.

Small Talk

This feature presents a natural conversation that incorporates a grammar point from the unit and is followed by an exercise or an activity that allows students to practice the language.

Model the conversation with a more advanced student.

Partnerwork

This feature is a two-page information-gap activity. Students work together in pairs. Each person has information that his or her partner does not have, and each person should look at his or her own page only. Students work together to obtain the information orally from their partners to complete their task.

Try to pair more advanced students with those who need extra practice. Have pairs of students compare their answers in a class session.

Use What You Know

This feature is a communicative activity that involves all four skills (listening, speaking, reading, and writing) and is based on a context from the unit.

In Your Own Words

This feature provides an opportunity for more communicative practice. Students work in pairs or small groups to complete an oral and/or written task involving their own personal information.

Wrapping Up

The final feature of the unit, Wrapping Up provides a summary practice with the most important grammar points presented in the unit.

Review Units

Periodic Review Units provide opportunities for freer, more communicative practice. Review Units are cumulative, and present previously introduced grammar points in interesting new contexts. Learner-generated stories are included that describe holidays in students' countries and important events in students' lives.

Teacher Script for Listening Exercises

Some grammar points are hard to distinguish in normal conversation. ("Was it singular or plural? Was it present or past tense?") Several listening exercises are included that relate to the grammar points presented. Students are asked to listen to the teacher and mark the answer that they hear. Once students can hear the difference between singular and plural or between past and present, it will be easier for them to say the difference.

Listening Exercises are preceded by listening and writing icons. Refer to the Teacher Script pages 161–163. Be sure to read the teacher script as naturally as possible, allowing for the particular needs of your students.

Appendix

The Appendix provides detailed information along with mini-exercises on pronunciation and spelling of selected grammar points. It also includes useful vocabulary, such as weights and measures and two-word verbs. See the *Book 3 Teacher's Edition* for information on when and how to present the material.

Answer Key

Answers for all written exercises are provided in the Answer Key beginning on page 178. Each teacher's edition includes a complete answer key for all the exercises in the corresponding student book.

Successful Language Learning

Language learning is enhanced when students are actively and cheerfully engaged in the learning process. Sometimes students may prefer not to offer personal information about themselves. Sensitivity to their feelings is the best guide. Let students know that they can use fictitious information if they prefer.

The most important factor for success is to create a classroom atmosphere in which learning is enjoyable and relatively stress free, so students feel safe yet challenged. Happy teaching!

> Look for grammar-guide pages, step-by-step teaching suggestions, and extension activities in *English Connections, Book 3 Teacher's Edition*.

> ♦ Simple Present
> ♦ Simple Present—Stative Verbs
> ♦ Simple Present vs. Present Continuous
> ♦ Meanings of *Have*

Unit 1 Who's that?

Where are these people? What are they doing? Talk about each person.

Setting the Scene

Ana: Are those your students, Jean?
Jean: Most of them. Do you see the students at the table? They're practicing their English. They practice every day before class. That's Gloria. She tells really interesting stories.
Ana: Who's that Asian woman?
Jean: That's Yoshiko. She's from Japan. I think she's having tea. Would you like some?
Ana: Sure.

Simple Present

Gloria **tells** interesting stories about Mexico.

| I You We They | **tell** | interesting stories. | **Does** | she | **tell** interesting stories? |

| He She | **tells** | interesting stories. | **Do** | we you I they | **tell** stories? |

You can use the simple present to talk about things you do as a habit.

> The -s ending sounds like /s/, /z/, or /iz/.

  1 Listen to the verbs. Put a check (✓) under the sound you hear.

	/s/	/z/	/iz/
1.	_____	_____	_____
2.	_____	_____	_____
3.	_____	_____	_____
4.	_____	_____	_____

2 Work with a partner. Plan to meet for one day every week to study together. Find out when you can meet.

Example: A: What do you do on Mondays?
B: I work every Monday until 3:30. What do you do on Tuesdays after 3:30?
A: My wife and I usually go shopping.

Make a chart showing the activities you and your partner do every day. Then decide when to meet and tell the class.

Focus on Vocabulary

Time Expressions

Jean: **How often** do you draw, Sergio?
Sergio: **Once or twice a week.**

every day	twice a day	three times a day
once a week	twice a week	three times a week
once a month	twice a month	three times a month
once a year	twice a year	three times a year

Jean: When do you run, Tan?
Tan: I run **on Saturdays**.
Jean: When do you draw, Sergio?
Sergio: **On the weekends**, usually.

| on Saturdays | in January | in the summer | in the fall |
| on the weekends | in July | in the winter | in the spring |

3 How often do you do these things and when? Ask a partner.

Example: do the laundry
A: How often do you *do the laundry*?
B: *Once a week.*
A: When?
B: *On Saturday afternoons.*

go to the grocery store   rent a video   visit your relatives
clean your house or   wash the dishes   watch TV
  apartment

4 Now tell the class or a small group two things about your partner.

Unit 1   3

Simple Present—Stative Verbs

I **have** a headache. (*now*) I **need** some aspirin. (*now*)
I **see** my students. (*now*) I **know** their names. (*now*)

Feelings	Thoughts	Senses	Relationships, Conditions
want	know	see	have
need	understand	hear	own
like	remember	smell	
hate			
prefer			

Stative verbs describe feelings, thoughts, senses, relationships, and conditions. They are used in the simple present, not the present continuous, even when you use them to talk about the present moment.

5 On the first day of class, Tan Nguyen had a terrible headache. After class, he went to a drugstore to buy some medicine. He talked to the pharmacist. Read this conversation he had with the pharmacist.

  Pharmacist: Can I help you?
  Tan Nguyen: Yes, I have a really bad *headache*. I need something for it, but I don't know what.
  Pharmacist: A *headache*? You need *aspirin*. Look in the corner, next to the sign. Do you see it?
  Tan Nguyen: Yes, thank you.

  Now practice this conversation with a partner. Substitute the following words and change roles.

    stomachache—milk of magnesia   cough—cough syrup

6 Here are some of the dishes on the menu of a famous restaurant. Do you like these foods? Ask a partner if he or she likes each of the foods. Then tell a group or the class about your partner.

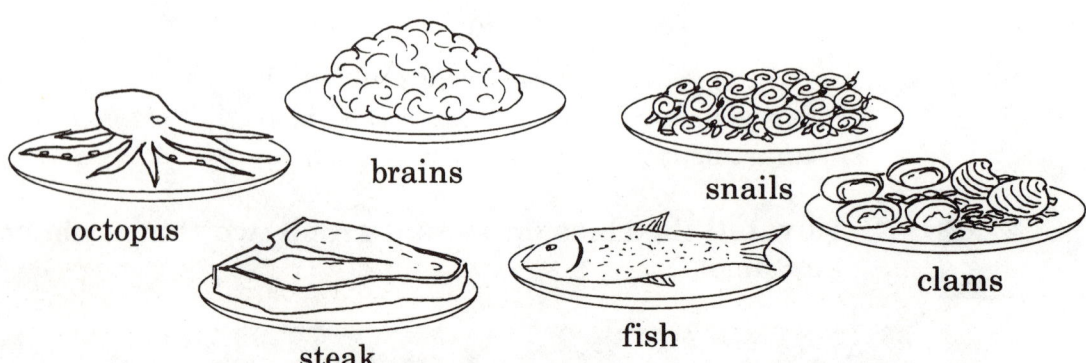

4

Unit 1

Connections: Talking About What You Don't Like

In the U.S., when someone offers you something you don't like, don't say, "No, I don't like that." Instead say, "No, thank you." If someone asks, "Don't you like it?" you can say, "No, not really. But thank you anyway."

When there are several choices and one choice is something you like, you can say, "Thank you, I prefer _____."

 7 Work with a partner. Take turns offering and refusing the following foods. Use the conversation as a model and substitute the foods listed below.

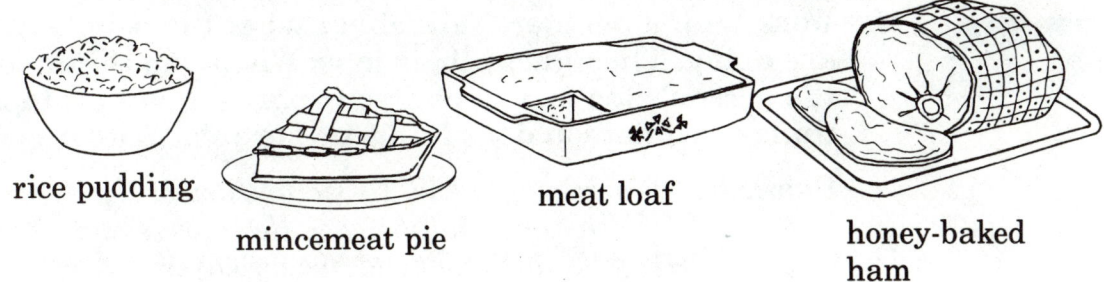

rice pudding mincemeat pie meat loaf honey-baked ham

Jean: This *cranberry sauce* is delicious! Have some.
Yoshiko: No, thank you.
Jean: Don't you like *cranberry sauce*?
Yoshiko: No, not really. But thank you anyway.

  8 Think of foods you *like*, *don't like*, and *hate*. Tell a partner about them.

Example: *I like strawberries and pineapple. I don't like canned vegetables. I hate canned fish.*

Unit 1

Simple Present vs. Present Continuous

Gloria's **talking** to Victor. She **tells** really interesting stories.
Victor's **drinking** a cup of coffee. He **drinks** a cup of coffee before class every day.
Jean's **teaching** her English class now. She **teaches** four evenings each week.
Chan Ho usually **takes** the bus to English class. But today he's **getting** a ride with Sergio.

Use the present continuous for things that you are doing now. Use the simple present to talk about a repeated or habitual situation.

> Time expressions often indicate that something is repeated or a habit.

9 Listen to your teacher. Your teacher will read sentences about several people. Circle the verb in each sentence.

1. runs	is running	6. smokes	is smoking
2. runs	is running	7. speaks	is speaking
3. has	is having	8. speaks	is speaking
4. washes	is washing	9. reads	is reading
5. smokes	is smoking	10. comes	is coming

10 Work with a partner. Talk about what the people in these pictures are doing. Then guess their jobs. When you think you know what the person's job is, you and your partner can brainstorm a list of things that person does in his or her job. Write down your ideas.

Example: *He's driving a bus. He's a bus driver. He takes people to work. He drives around the city. He collects money from passengers. He gives the money to his employer.*

Unit 1

11 Make a list of five jobs you know about. Do not show your list to your classmates. Then take turns acting out one of the jobs on your list in front of the class. Your classmates can ask you questions to find out what your job is.

Example: A: Are you washing clothes?
B: No, I'm not.
C: Are you washing the dishes?
B: No, but I'm washing something.
D: Are you washing a baby?
A: Yes, I'm a nurse.

12 Work with a partner and role-play the following situations: *making a table, cooking a steak, making a chocolate sundae.* Tell your partner what you are doing and what you need.

Example: Your partner: What are you doing?
You: I'm *making a table.* I'm *making the legs now.*
Your partner: Do you have everything?
You: No, I *need more wood.*

Table: making the legs
need more wood

Steak: putting the sauce on
need more sauce

Sundae: adding ice cream
need more chocolate

13 Complete each of the following sentences with the correct form of the verb in parentheses. Put the verbs into the simple present or the present continuous.

1. Ali always _____ (*fix*) his car in his uncle's garage.
   Right now he _____ (*install*) new brakes.

2. Chan Ho _____ (*own*) a restaurant.
   He _____ (*have*) a lot of customers on the weekends.

3. Chan Ho Cho is busy now. He _____ (*talk*) to some customers in his restaurant. He always _____ (*greet*) new customers.

4. Sergio sometimes _____ (*draw*) pictures of his friends and relatives. He _____ (*draw*) his niece now.

5. Masha _____ (*read*) three newspapers every day.
   I _____ (*not read*) any.

6. The students _____ (*practice*) their English every day.
   They _____ (*know*) it will help them.

Unit 1

Meanings of Have

Stative

Wes **has** a nice car. (*possession*)   Maria **has** a cold. (*condition*)

Active

Carlos **has** breakfast every morning at seven.
Carlos **is having** breakfast right now.
(*consumption*—eating, drinking, etc.)

Typical uses of have as an active verb:

have breakfast	have dinner	have a drink
have lunch	have coffee	have dessert

> Stative *have*: simple present
> Active *have*: simple present or present continuous

   14 Work in a group. In turns, ask what the others in your group usually have for breakfast. Make a list of these foods for each person. Include the things that each person has to drink at breakfast (*coffee, tea, milk, juice,* etc.).

Example: Student 1: Sasha, what do you usually have for breakfast?
Sasha: I have two eggs and a cup of tea for breakfast. What do you have for breakfast?

  15 With your group, write the foods and beverages from Exercise 14 on separate cards. Put all of the cards in a bag. Choose one card. Mime the action of eating or drinking the item on your card. The others in your group ask you yes/no questions to guess what you are having. They must guess correctly within four questions.

Example: A: Are you having a cup of coffee?
B: No, I'm not.
C: Are you having a glass of juice?
B: Yes, I am.
D: Are you having a glass of orange juice?
B: No, I'm not.

16 Use the correct form of *have* to write sentences about the people in these pictures.

1. Salar  a broken arm

2. Hanh  ice cream (now)

3. Miguel and Juana  a house

4. Tanya  lunch in the cafeteria (every day)

Write your sentences on a separate sheet of paper. Compare sentences with a partner.

Partnerwork ▶ Person A

Work with a partner. Person A looks at this page only. Person B looks at page 10 only. Who are the people in the picture below? Ask your partner questions to find out the names you don't know. Write the names on the lines below.

Example: A: Who is *putting on lipstick*?
B: That's *Helena Wolinska*.
A: How do you spell that?
B: *H-E-L-E-N-A W-O-L-I-N-S-K-A*

Unit 1   9

Partnerwork ▶ Person B

Work with a partner. Person B looks at this page only. Person A looks at page 9 only. Who are the people in the picture below? Ask your partner questions to find out the names you don't know. Write the names on the lines below.

Example: A: Who is *reading the newspaper?*
B: That's *Sergio Long.*
A: How do you spell that?
B: *S-E-R-G-I-O L-O-N-G*

In Your Own Words

Write a letter to a friend in your native country. Tell your friend about some of the things you do every day in the U.S., and write about what you are doing today in class. Also, tell your friend about the things people don't have in the U.S. that you have in your native country. Read your letter to the class.

Wrapping Up

In a group, write an article about life in the U.S. for people who are coming here to visit. Write about things people do or have in the U.S. that are different from your country.

Example: *Americans don't usually take their shoes off when they enter a person's house. In my country, we take our shoes off and put on slippers when we enter a person's house.*

10 Unit 1

> ♦ Simple Past of Regular and Irregular Verbs
> ♦ *Used to*
> ♦ *Used to:* Wh-Questions
> ♦ *Not . . . anymore*
> ♦ *But*
> ♦ *Didn't use to*

Unit 2   I used to work for a magazine

Jean's friend Ana is talking to Jean's class. What do you think her job is?

Setting the Scene

Ana: Jean asked me to talk to you about my job. I'm a writer.
Helena: Do you like your job?
Ana: I love it. I used to work for a magazine, but I didn't like that. I didn't use to have any real freedom. But that's not a problem anymore. Now I work at home.
Tan: Do you work on a computer?
Ana: Yes. I used to work on a typewriter. But now I work on a computer.

Simple Past of Regular and Irregular Verbs

ask → **asked**
Helena **asked** Ana about her job.

come → **came**
Ana **came** to Jean's class.

| I
you
he
she | asked | we
you
they | asked | I
you
he
she | came | we
you
they | came |

Did Amir **ask** Ana about her job?
No, he didn't.

Did Ana **come** to Jean's class?
Yes, she did.

See pages 164–167 of the Appendix for a review of the rules, pronunciation, and forms of irregular verbs.

> Regular verbs add *-ed* in the past.

 1 Think of three things you did yesterday and write them below.

  1. _____
  2. _____
  3. _____

 2 Tell your partner where you lived five years ago.

  Example: *Five years ago I lived in Mexico City.*

  Now tell the class about your partner.

12 Unit 2

3 In a group, talk about how long you lived in your previous house or apartment. Write your answers and tell the class.

Example: *I lived in my apartment in Brooklyn for six months.*

Used to

Ana **used to** hate her job. (Now she has a new job, and she likes it.)

Victor **used to** play soccer every day in school. (He isn't in school anymore. He doesn't play soccer every day anymore.)

I You He She	**used to**	play soccer in school.	They We	**used to**	play soccer in school.

Use *used to* for things you did in the past but don't do now.

4 Think of four things you used to do when you were a child. Write sentences with *used to*.

Example: *I used to play in the park.*

1. _____
2. _____
3. _____
4. _____

5 Think of two things you did before you came to the United States that you don't do anymore. Write them on the lines below. Then tell a partner about them.

Example: *I used to sell vegetables at the market.*

Before   **Now**

1. _____   _____
2. _____   _____

Unit 2   13

Used to: Wh-Questions

Tan, **what** did you use to do in Vietnam?
I **used to** be a taxi driver.

Jean, **where** did you use to teach?
I **used to** teach in Turkey.

In questions, there is no *d* on the end of the verb *use*.

 6 Work with a partner. Look at the pictures below and ask what each person used to do and what he or she does now. Take turns asking and answering.

Example: A: What did Pedro use to do?
B: He used to be a factory worker.
A: What does he do now?
B: Now he's a cook.

Masha   **Fu**

Before   Now   Before   Now

engineer   waitress   farm worker   restaurant manager

  7 In groups, ask each other what you used to do in your native country. Answer with your information from Exercise 5.

Example: A: Chan Ho, what did you use to do in Korea?
B: I was a farmer. I used to raise chickens and sell eggs at the market. I also used to grow rice and millet.

Now decide which thing is most interesting for each person. Tell the class about it.

Small Talk: What do you do?

In the U.S., people often ask, "What do you do?" when they mean, "What's your job?" This is a common question people ask when they first meet. It's a subject that most people can talk about easily.

Here are some ways to answer this question:

I work **in a hospital**.	OR	**I'm a nurse.**
I work **in a dentist's office**.	OR	**I'm a dental assistant.**
I work **in a restaurant**.	OR	**I'm a waiter.**

If you don't have a job, you can say, "I'm not working right now" OR "I'm unemployed."

If you have children and you don't work, you can say, "I stay home with my children."

---

 8 Work with a partner. Ask your partner what he or she does now and what he or she used to do (before coming to the U.S.). Practice answering these questions with the answer types in the Small Talk section.

    Example: A: What do you do, Maria?
                  B: I work in an office. OR I'm a secretary.
                  A: What did you use to do?
                  B: I used to work in a school. OR I used to be a teacher.

  9 In a group, write the jobs you do and the jobs you used to do on separate cards and put them face down. Each student chooses two cards. Follow the example dialogue for Exercise 8 and answer with the jobs written on your cards.

Unit 2

Focus on Vocabulary

Adjectives That Describe Feelings

When change is bad, people feel **sad**, **scared**, or **discouraged**.
When change is good, people feel **excited**, **happy**, or **grateful**.

Warsaw, Poland—1990

San Jose, California—Today

Helena used to be an opera singer.

Now she works in a factory. She feels **sad**.

scared

discouraged

happy

sad

10 Look at the pictures. Write what each person used to do. Then write what the person does now. Finally, write how you think the person feels about the change.

Tacoma, Washington—1989

Tucson, Arizona—Today

1. Victor _____. But now _____.

He feels _____.

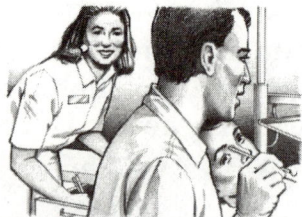

Hermosillo, Mexico—1993

San Antonio, Texas—Today

2. Gloria _____. But now _____.

She feels _____.

Not... anymore

We used to have a big house. Now we live in an apartment.
We do **not** have a big house **anymore**.

We do**n't** have a big house **anymore**.

Jean used to have an old black-and-white TV. Now she has a color TV.
She does**n't** have her old black-and-white TV **anymore**.

Sergio used to live in Peru. Now he lives in the U.S.
He does**n't** live in Peru **anymore**.

You can use *not ... anymore* to talk about something that is finished or a situation in the past that is not true now.

Anymore usually goes at the end of a sentence or clause.

11 Look at your answers for Exercise 4, on page 13. Using those answers, write four sentences with *not ... anymore*.

Example: *I don't play in the park anymore.*

1. _____
2. _____
3. _____
4. _____

12 What did you do in your native country before you came to the U.S.? With a partner, talk about the things that you don't do anymore.

Example: *I don't sell eggs at the market anymore.*

13 Listen to people talk about their jobs. Circle the sentence that means the same as the information you hear.

1. She's a dental assistant.   She isn't a dental assistant anymore.
2. She's a factory worker.   She isn't a factory worker anymore.
3. He's a real estate agent.   He isn't a real estate agent anymore.
4. He's a farm worker.   He isn't a farm worker anymore.
5. She's a police officer.   She isn't a police officer anymore.

But

I **used to** take the bus to work.   **But** now I drive.
I **used to** live in an apartment.   **But** now I live in a house.

Use *used to* to compare things you did before with things you do now.
Use *but* to show the difference.

I **used to** teach English.   **But** now I teach Spanish.
I **used to** work on Saturdays.   **But** now I have a different job.

> In this context, use *used to*, not the simple past.

14 Think about yourself. How have you changed over the years? On a separate sheet of paper, write sentences about the way you were and the way you are now. Then tell the class about your past. They will guess how you are different now.

Example: A: I used to live in a little village near the sea.
B: But now you live in a big city near a noisy highway!
A: That's right!

Past
I used to live in a little village near the sea.

Present
But now I live in a big city.

15 Work with a partner. Practice the conversation. Then substitute the phrases below and change roles.

A: I used to be *afraid at home alone*.
     But I'm not *afraid* anymore.
B: That's great! How did you do it?
A: I *got a big dog*.

1. 100 pounds overweight/started working out and eating less
2. late for everything/set my watch 10 minutes ahead
3. sick all the time/quit smoking
4. exhausted every evening/started getting more sleep

16 Now write your own conversation with your partner. You can use the conversation from Exercise 15 as a model. Act out your conversation for the class.

Didn't use to

I **didn't use to** eat pizza. But now I eat pizza all the time.
She **didn't use to** exercise. But now she runs two miles a day.

I	**didn't use to** eat pizza.	We	**didn't use to** eat pizza.
You		You	
He		They	
She			

Use *didn't use to* for things you never did in the past but that you do now.

> In speaking, we often use the contraction *didn't*.

17 Gloria writes in her journal every night. Last night she wrote about how her life has changed since she moved to the U.S. Read what she wrote.

> Wednesday, Sept. 6
>
> I can't believe how different my life is now. For one thing, I didn't use to pay with checks. I didn't even have a checking account. But now I write checks for everything.
>
> Of course, I didn't use to write in English. I couldn't even speak much English. But now I write in English in my journal every night. My wonderful teacher, Jean, tells me not to worry about spelling, just write. So, that's what I do.

18 Think of four things you didn't use to do before you came to the U.S. that you do now. Make sentences about these things with *didn't use to*.

Example: *I didn't use to drive a car. But now I drive every day.*

1. _____
2. _____
3. _____
4. _____

19 Work in a group. Talk about the four things from Exercise 18 that you didn't use to do. Discuss your feelings about the changes. Then report about your classmates to the class.

Example:
A: I didn't use to drive in Japan. But now I live in America, and I drive everywhere. But I don't like to drive.
B: Yoshiko never used to drive in Japan. In America, she drives, but she doesn't like it.

In Your Own Words

On the lines below, write about how your life has changed since you came to this country. Use Gloria's journal from Exercise 17 as a model. Exchange books with a partner and read your classmates' writing.

_____
_____
_____
_____
_____
_____
_____
_____

Wrapping Up

Write three sentences about yourself—two true and one false. Stand in front of the class and read your three sentences. The class can ask five questions to decide which sentence is false.

> ♦ Past Participles: Regular and Irregular
> ♦ Pronunciation of Past Participles
> ♦ Present Perfect
> ♦ Present Perfect with *Never* and *Always*

Unit 3 Have you ever changed a tire?

Where are Ana and Jean? What happened to the car? What are they going to do?

Unit 3   21

Setting the Scene

Ana: I've never seen anything like this. Arizona's great!
Jean: I know! I love the open space! We haven't seen anyone for an hour!
Ana: What was that?
Jean: Oh, no! We hit a rock! We got a flat tire! Have you ever changed a tire?
Ana: No, I haven't.
Jean: I guess we're going to learn.

Past Participles: Regular and Irregular

I've never **changed** a tire. Have you?

	Simple Past	*Past Participle*
change	changed	changed
fix	fixed	fixed

I've never **done** that.

	Simple Past	*Past Participle*
do	did	done
go	went	gone

See Appendix page 168 for a list of irregular past participles.

For most regular and irregular verbs, the simple-past form and past-participle forms are the same. For some irregular verbs, the past and the past-participle forms are different.

1   Think of four things you would like to do. Ask a partner if he or she has done these things. Use *have* + a past participle.

Example: A: Have you ever taken a vacation with a friend?
B: Yes, I have. OR No, I haven't.

2   Fill in the simple-past and past-participle forms of these verbs.

Simple	Past	Past Participle
1. invite	_____	_____
2. visit	_____	_____
3. watch	_____	_____
4. study	_____	_____

3 Fill in the past-participle forms of these irregular verbs. If you need help, use the list of irregular past participles on Appendix page 168.

	Simple	Past	Past Participle
1.	do	did	_____
2.	have	had	_____
3.	go	went	_____
4.	eat	ate	_____
5.	am/is/are	was/were	_____

Pronunciation of Past Participles

1 syllable: live—**lived** (*livd*) stop—**stopped** (*stopt*)

The *-ed* in past and past-participle forms of regular verbs is pronounced like a quick /t/ or /d/ sound.

2 syllables: paint—**painted** (*pain*-tid) need—**needed** (*nee*-did)

When the present form of the verb ends with /t/ or /d/, add an extra syllable.

 4 Listen, write the words, and write the number of syllables.

Example: *wanted* 2

1. _____   5. _____
2. _____   6. _____
3. _____   7. _____
4. _____   8. _____

 5 Brainstorm a list of regular past participles. Write them on the board. Put them into three columns: those with a /t/ sound, those with a /d/ sound, and those with an extra syllable, /id/.

 6 Practice repeating each past participle after your teacher as a whole class. Then divide into groups and continue to practice. Your teacher will listen to you in your group.

Unit 3

Present Perfect

I **have** never **changed** a tire.

Have you ever **changed** a tire?   Yes, I **have**. **Have** you?

Has he | ever **changed** a tire?   No, he **hasn't**.
she | Yes, she **has**.

Have they ever **been** to Disneyland?   Yes, they **have**.
we   No, we **haven't**.

You can use the present perfect (*have* + past participle) to ask people about their experiences at a nonspecific time in their lives before the present.

    7 Listen to your teacher. Circle the verbs you hear.

1. has gone   have gone
2. has done   have done
3. has worked   have worked
4. has lived   have lived

   8 Tan and Sergio are skiing in Aspen. With a partner, ask and answer questions about Tan and Sergio. Ask, "Have they ever . . . ?" Ask about the following things:

take ski lessons   break a leg   use ski poles

9 Work in pairs. Have you or your partner ever done these things? Write a question about the activity on the line below each picture. Then ask and answer questions about these activities.

Example: A: Have you ever changed a tire?
B: No, I haven't. OR Yes, I have.

1. change a tire

_____
_____
_____

2. work on a car

_____
_____
_____

3. paint a room

_____
_____
_____

4. eat egg rolls

_____
_____
_____

5. go to an art museum

_____
_____
_____

6. have surgery

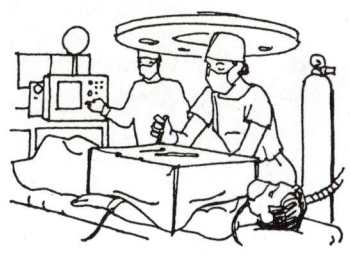

_____
_____
_____

Present Perfect with *Never* and *Always*

| I | have never been to Tokyo. | I
You
We
They | 've never been to Tokyo. |

| He
She | has never been to Tokyo. | He
She | 's never been to Tokyo. |

I've always wanted to go there.

For things you haven't done at any time in your life, you can use the present perfect with *never*. For things you have never done but want to do, you can use the present perfect with *always*.

10 Think of four things you've never done. Write these things on the lines below.

Example: *I've never ridden a horse.*

1. _____
2. _____
3. _____
4. _____

11 In groups, talk about the things you've never done. As a group, decide which one thing is the most interesting for each person. Then tell the class about these things.

Example: *Sergio has never played hockey.*
Tan has never eaten a hamburger.
Yoshiko has never seen the Atlantic Ocean.
Gloria has never dyed her hair.

12 What are four things you've never done but always wanted to do? Write them on the lines below.

Example: *I've always wanted to go to Africa.*

1. _____
2. _____
3. _____
4. _____

Focus on Vocabulary

Sports

In a group, discuss these questions about each picture: 1. Is this a popular sport in your native country? 2. Have you ever played this sport? You can make notes on the lines below.

1. soccer

2. racquetball

3. baseball

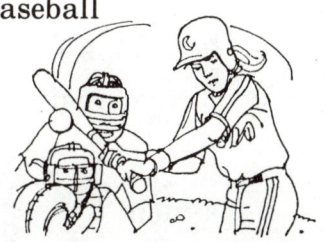

4. golf

5. volleyball

6. hockey

7. basketball

8. football

13 Work in a group. Fill in the chart with the names of the sports from the vocabulary box on page 27. Then discuss the similarities (things that are the same) and differences (things that are different) in the charts in your group.

Sports I've played	Sports I've always wanted to play	Sports I've never played
_____	_____	_____
_____	_____	_____
_____	_____	_____
_____	_____	_____
_____	_____	_____

14 Every culture and country has its favorite foods. Have you ever had these foods? Fill in the last lines with two other countries and foods. Include your native country if it is not on the list.

Country	Food
1. Russia	borscht, pirozhki, black caviar
2. Poland	pierogis, punchki
3. Cuba	flan, rice and black beans
4. Korea	kimchi
5. Mexico	tortillas, enchiladas
6. Morocco	couscous, tajine
7. Japan	sushi, sashimi, sukiyaki
8. China	wonton, chicken satay
9. India	samosas, tandoori lamb
10. _____	_____
11. _____	_____

15 In groups, talk about the foods above. Here are some suggestions for starting your conversations.

Example: What's borscht? Have you ever eaten it? What does it taste like?

28   Unit 3

Connections: Continuing a Conversation

Sometimes people will ask you about your experiences and your answer will be no. Here are two ways to continue the conversation:

1. A: Irina, have you ever been to *Michigan*?
   B: No, but I've been to *Illinois*.
   A: Oh, really? Where in *Illinois*?

2. A: Have you ever been to *Washington, D.C.*?
   B: No, but I've always wanted to go there. Have you ever been there?
   A: Yes, I have. OR No, I haven't.

16 With a partner, practice the conversations above. Then use your own ideas for the names of the places. For countries or states, use the first conversation as a model. For cities, use the second conversation.

Partnerwork ▶ Person A

Person A looks at this page only. Person B looks at page 30 only. Look at the map of the United States. Write *A* in each state you have been to. Write *a* in six other states you've never been to but always wanted to visit. Then find out what states your partner has been to. Write *B* in these states. Also, find out what states your partner has always wanted to visit. Write *b* in these states. Ask questions like the one below the map.

Example: A: Have you ever been to Maine?
B: Yes, I have.
A: I've never been there. Tell me about it.

Unit 3   29

Partnerwork ▶ Person B

Person B looks at this page only. Person A looks at page 29 only. Look at the map of the United States. Write *B* in each state you have been to. Write *b* in six other states you've never been to but always wanted to visit. Then find out what states your partner has been to. Write *A* in these states. Also, find out what states your partner has always wanted to visit. Write *a* in these states. Ask questions like the one below the map.

Example: A: Have you ever been to Maine?
B: Yes, I have.
A: I've never been there. Tell me about it.

Use What You Know

What are the advantages and disadvantages of living in the country? What are the advantages and disadvantages of living in a big city? Which do you prefer? Why? Discuss these questions with a partner. Then write down some of your ideas on a separate sheet of paper and share them with the class.

Example: *I have always wanted to live in the country.*
I have never liked living in big cities. They are too noisy.

Wrapping Up

Write about the things you have studied and the things you have learned this year. Also, write about the things you have never studied but have always wanted to study.

Review: Units 1–3

1. Work with a partner. Look at the pictures below. Talk about what each person is doing. Then guess how often each person does this activity. Write your answers on the lines below.

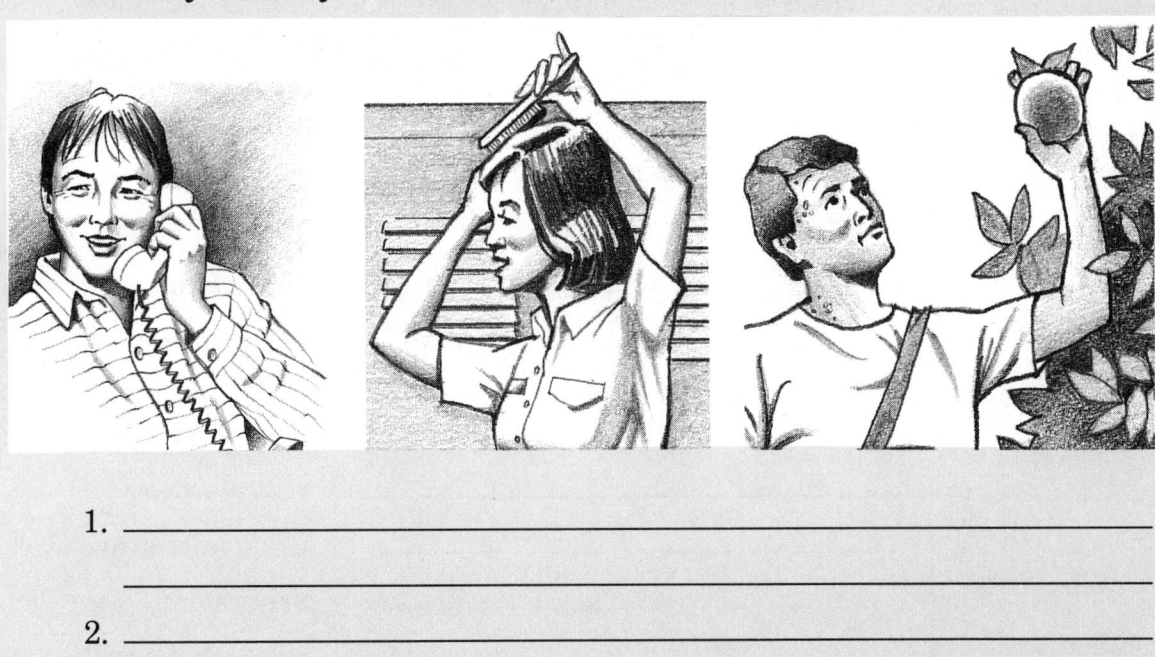

   1. _____
   2. _____
   3. _____

2. Work with a partner. Talk about your childhood. Write three things you did at a specific time or day and three other things you used to do but don't do now. For the things you used to do, make sentences with *used to*, *but*, and *not . . . anymore*.

   Example: *On my tenth birthday, I went to the circus with my parents. I used to take music lessons, but I don't anymore.*

   Things I did at a specific time or day
   1. _____
   2. _____
   3. _____

   Things I used to do but don't do anymore
   1. _____
   2. _____
   3. _____

3. Find someone who has done each of the things listed below. When someone answers yes to a question, write his or her name next to those words. Find a different name for each thing.

Example: Have you ever played the guitar?
Yes, I have. OR No, I haven't.

Name	Question
_____	play the guitar
_____	work in a restaurant
_____	change the oil in a car
_____	feel embarrassed about your English
_____	have a job interview
_____	rent a video
_____	use a microwave oven
_____	drive a car
_____	ride a motorcycle
_____	buy something at a garage sale
_____	read a book in English
_____	take a computer class
_____	run out of gas
_____	write a poem in English
_____	meet a famous person
_____	break a bone
_____	find money in the street
_____	go to a baseball game
_____	ride a horse

- ♦ Present Perfect with Time Expressions
- ♦ Present Perfect vs. Simple Past

Unit 4 How long have you lived here?

Why are Jean's students working in pairs? What do you think they're talking about?

Setting the Scene

Helena: Tan, how long have you lived here?
Tan: Well, my family and I left Vietnam ten years ago.
Helena: Oh, then you've lived here for ten years.
Tan: No. First we lived in a refugee camp in Thailand.
Helena: How long did you live there?
Tan: For about a year.
Helena: Then how long have you lived in the U.S.?
Tan: We've lived here since 1993. Before that, we lived in France.

Present Perfect with Time Expressions

Tan and his family **have lived** in Los Angeles **for almost a year**.

| I / You / We / They | **have lived** | here **for a year**. | He / She | **has lived** | here **for a year**. |

Statements: He**'s studied** English **for five months**.
He**'s studied** English **since March**.
Wh-question: How long **has he studied** English?
Yes/no question: **Have you lived** here for a long time?
Short answers: Yes, **I have.** OR No, **I haven't.**

For indicates how long you have done something. *Since* indicates the specific time you started doing something.

You can use the present perfect (*have* + past participle) for things that started in the past and continue in the present.

1 Work with a partner. Take turns asking and answering questions about your life and your partner's life. Use the present perfect.

Example: A: How long have you worked at your job?
B: I've worked at my job for two months.

1. work at your job
2. drive a car
3. live in your house or apartment
4. study English
5. live in this city or town

34 Unit 4

2 Finish these sentences about yourself.

1. I've lived in the United States since _____.

2. I've lived here for _____.

3. I've studied English since _____.

4. I've studied English for _____.

3 Work with a partner. Create conversations like the ones below. Use your answers from Exercise 2.

Example: (*It's November now.*)
- A: I've lived in the U.S. since August. So I've only lived here for about three months. What about you?
- B: I've lived in this country since March. So I've lived here for about eight months.

4 When Tan Nguyen went to the immigration office, the immigration officer asked him a lot of questions. Read their conversation.

- Officer: How long have you lived in the U.S.?
- Tan: I haven't lived here for very long. I've lived here since last August.
- Officer: So you've lived here for about a year.
- Tan: That's right.
- Officer: Do you have a job?
- Tan: Yes, I'm working in a warehouse.
- Officer: How long have you worked there?
- Tan: About five months.
- Officer: So you've worked there since February.
- Tan: Yes. Now I'm studying English. I've studied English for about two months.
- Officer: Two months? So you've studied English since May?
- Tan: That's correct.

Practice this conversation with a partner. Then role-play yourself and the immigration officer. Add your own information. If you don't have a job, the immigration officer can ask, "How long have you been unemployed?"

Unit 4   35

Focus on Vocabulary

Time Expressions with *For* and *Since*

Use *for* with time expressions like these, for a period of time.

for a long time
for five years
for three months
for a few days

for two hours
for fifteen minutes
for thirty seconds

Use *since* with time expressions like these, which give a starting time.

since childhood
since 1992
since September
since last summer

since yesterday
since six o'clock
since this morning

NOT *since five years, *since three months

5 Read these sentences. Write *for* or *since* on the lines.

1. Norma has worked at the coffee shop _____ a long time.

2. Manuel has lived in the U.S. _____ two years.

3. Ewa's worked at a factory _____ six months.

4. Jean's had a cold _____ a week.

5. I've had a headache _____ last night.

6. I've had a headache _____ twelve hours.

7. Mei's been in the U.S. _____ April.

6 Guess the answers to these questions.

1. Who in your class do you think has studied English for the longest time? Write his or her name: _____

2. Who do you think has studied English for the shortest time? Write his or her name: _____

7 Now, see if your guesses in Exercise 6 were right. Find out by asking your classmates, "How long have you studied English?" Then form a line according to how long you have studied English—from the shortest time to the longest time.

Small Talk: How long have you been here?

In the United States when people meet you for the first time, they often ask,

> How long have you lived in the United States? OR
> How long have you been in the United States?

A: How long have you lived in the United States?
B: I've lived in the U.S. for two years.
(I came to the U.S. two years ago. I'm living in the U.S. now.)

> I've lived here for two years.
> I've been here for two years.

You can also use short answers:
A: How long have you lived in the United States?
B: For two years. OR Two years.

8 Victor Fuentes came to the United States in 1989. He's lived here since then. Here are some things he bought in the U.S. and when he bought them.

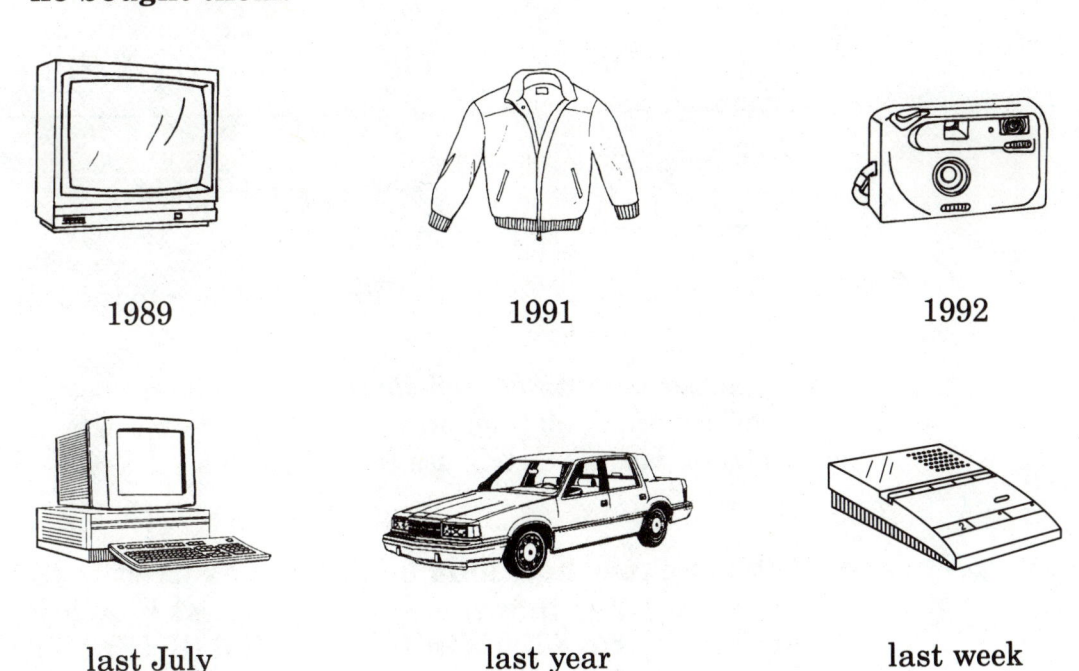

| 1989 | 1991 | 1992 |

| last July | last year | last week |

How long has Victor had each of these things? Take turns asking and answering questions with a partner. Use short answers with *for* and *since*.

Example: A: How long has Victor had a color TV?
B: Since 1989. OR For _____ years.

Unit 4   37

9. What are three things you bought in the U.S. that you didn't have before? Write the names of these things on three cards.

Example:

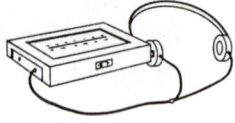

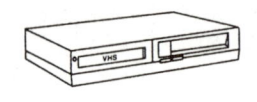

Walkman   VCR   answering machine

Exchange cards with a partner. How long has your partner had each of the things on his or her cards? Take turns asking and answering questions.

Example: One of Student B's cards: Walkman

- A: How long have you had a Walkman?
- B: *Since last year.* OR *For one year.*
- A: How do you like it?
- B: I like *it* a lot. *I listen to music. It helps my English.*

Present Perfect vs. Simple Past

2 years — Now   2 years ago — Now

I've lived in the U.S. **for two years**.   I **came** to the U.S. **two years ago**.

Time expressions with *for* and *since* and the present perfect tell you that this time continues into the present. With past-time expressions (such as *ago* or *last week, last year,* etc.), use the simple past.

10. Ask a partner how long he or she has lived in the U.S. Make a chart with this information. Then guess how long four other classmates have lived in the U.S. Add their names and your guesses to your chart.

11. Check your guesses from Exercise 10. Ask your classmates if the time on your chart is right.

    Example: A: Pierre, have you lived here for two years?
    - B: No, I've lived here for five months.
    - A: Oh, then you came here in March.
    - B: That's right.

12 Look at this picture. How long has each person lived in the U.S.? How long has each person worked here? With a partner, ask and answer the questions below about each person.

Example: A: How long has Amir lived here?
B: He's lived here for _____.
A: When did he come to the U.S.?
B: He came here _____.

A: How long has Amir worked here?
B: He's worked here for _____.
A: When did he start work?
B: He started work _____.

Amir — 2 YEARS IN THIS COUNTRY. 10 MONTHS ON THE JOB.
Yoshiko — 10 MONTHS IN THIS COUNTRY. 5 MONTHS ON THE JOB.
Helena — 4 YEARS IN THIS COUNTRY. 3½ YEARS ON THE JOB.
Ana — 15 YEARS IN THIS COUNTRY. 10 YEARS ON THE JOB.

13 Fill in each blank with the correct form of the verb, simple past or present perfect. Check your answers with a partner.

Sergio Long __has had__ (have) an interesting life. He _____ (be) born in Peru to Chinese immigrants. When Sergio _____ (be) a teenager, his family _____ (decide) to move to the U.S. for better job opportunities. They _____ (live) in San Francisco for five years now. Sergio _____ (study) English and art since that time. Sergio is a very talented artist. He _____ (have) his artwork on display many times at his adult school and the local library. Last year he also _____ (help) other students paint a mural in the lobby of the school's new building.

Unit 4

14 Who do you think has lived in the U.S. for the longest and for the shortest time? Write your classmates' names and the reason for your guess.

1. I think _____ has lived in the U.S. for the longest time because _____.

2. I think _____ has lived in the U.S. for the shortest time because _____.

15 Form a line from the person who has been in the U.S. the shortest time to the person who has been in the U.S. the longest time. Each student tells the class how long he or she has lived in the U.S. (using *for* or *since*) and when he or she came here.

Example:
A: How long have you lived in this country?
B: For three years. OR Since _____.
A: When did you come here?
B: I came here _____.

I've lived in the United States for six months. I came here six months ago.

16 In a group, write the verbs *study, live, work, have, come, start, be,* and *leave* on separate cards and put them in a bag. Pick a card and make a sentence with the present perfect or the simple past. Another student will ask you a question with the same verb.

Example: (*start*)   A: I started work two years ago.
B: Did you start work in May?

(*work*)   A: I haven't worked in the U.S.
B: Where did you work before?

Connections: I haven't done that since . . .

There are things you used to do in the past but don't do anymore. There are places where you used to go. But you don't go to those places anymore. How long has it been?

I haven't read a newspaper since they decided to print cartoons.

Use this pattern:

I/we/you/they   haven't _____ + since + simple past

he/she/it   hasn't _____

Carlos **hasn't played** football **since** he **finished** high school.
Agnaldo **hasn't had** good feijoada **since** he **left** Brazil.
Sami **hasn't eaten** good couscous **since** he **left** Tunisia.
Seryozha and Valya **haven't had** sturgeon **since** they **left** Russia.
Deepa **hasn't seen** an Indian movie **since** she **came** to the U.S.

17 Think about some things you haven't done in a long time. Complete the following three sentences.

1. I haven't eaten _____

   since I _____.

2. I haven't seen _____

   since I _____.

3. I haven't _____

   since _____.

Now share your sentences with a group. What is the most interesting thing about each person? Decide together. Then tell the class.

Example: *Rosa hasn't had any free time since she had her baby.*

In Your Own Words

Imagine that you are applying for a job. The employer asks you about your work experience. Tell what you did in your native country and what you've done in the U.S. Make up a job history if necessary.

Example:

In Mexico, after I graduated from high school, I attended a technical college to get my dental hygienist training. I worked for a dentist for six years before I came here. In this country, I've worked as a waitress for a year. I've also studied English for six months.

Write your job history here.

_____

_____

_____

_____

_____

_____

Now, talk to a partner. Take turns role-playing job interviews as employer and applicant.

Wrapping Up

Find classmates who have done each of the things below. When someone answers yes, write in his or her name to complete the sentence. Find a different name for each thing.

Example: A: Have you been home to visit since moving to the U.S.?
B: Yes. I've been back once.
A: I'm sorry, I forgot your name.
B: It's Yoshiko.
A: How do you spell that?
B: Y-O-S-H-I-K-O
A: Thank you, Yoshiko.

Name

_____ has been home to visit since moving to the U.S.

_____ has lived in the U.S. for a long time.

_____ has been married for less than five years.

_____ has studied English since high school.

_____ has had the same address for two or more years.

- Commands and Requests
- Two-Word Verbs
- Two-Word Verbs (Separable and Inseparable)
- Two-Word Verbs with Pronouns

Unit 5   Would you pick that up, please?

LOCKER ROOM RULES
1. Pick up clean uniforms on Monday before 12:00 noon.
2. Drop off soiled uniforms on or before Sunday 12:00 noon.
3. Do not leave valuables in lockers.
4. Clean up after yourself.

YOUR MOTHER DOESN'T WORK HERE

Where is Gloria? What does she want to ask?

Setting the Scene

Gloria: Excuse me. Could you help me? Where's locker 25?
Delfina: It's right over there.
Gloria: Also, could you tell me something else? When do we drop off our dirty uniforms?
Delfina: On Sunday before noon.
Gloria: And when do we pick up our clean uniforms?
Delfina: On Monday before noon. It's all on the sign up there.

Commands and Requests

Commands
1. Urgent commands/warnings: **Watch** out!
2. Instructions for a process: **Add** two eggs and a cup of milk.
3. Telling someone what to do: **Open** your books to page three.
Turn down the stereo.

Informal Requests
David, | **can** / **will** | you turn down the stereo?

Formal Requests
Could / **Would** | you | show me how to do it?

Use can use *can* and *will* to make informal requests of friends and family. You can use *could* and *would* to make formal requests of strangers, bosses, or people you don't know well.

Don't use *to* after *can, will, could* or *would*.

1 Listen to these requests. Are they informal requests or formal requests? Put a check in the correct column.

Formal Requests	Informal Requests
1. _____	_____
2. _____	_____
3. _____	_____
4. _____	_____
5. _____	_____

2 Listen again. Now write the requests. Check your sentences with a partner.

1. _____
2. _____
3. _____
4. _____
5. _____

3 Use the requests from Exercise 2 as models to write your own requests. Think of requests you made last week. Share your new requests with a group.

Example: *Could you please help me open this door?*
Could you please help me with my homework?
Could you please help me read this map?

4 In a group write a request for each situation. Discuss whether to use a friendly or a polite request. Assign roles and practice a conversation for each situation. When you have practiced all the situations, present one to the class.

Example: *You are talking on the phone and your children are making a lot of noise. You want them to be quiet.*

Will you kids please be quiet? I'm on the phone.

1. The telephone rings, but you are busy. You want your husband/wife to answer it.

   _____

2. You forgot to bring a pen to class. You ask your classmate for a pen.

   _____

3. You are in line at the grocery store. You forgot to get eggs. You ask the person behind you in line to watch your cart while you get the eggs.

   _____

4. You are carrying a very heavy suitcase. You need to get on a bus. You ask a stranger for help.

   _____

5. Your co-worker wants to eat lunch with you. You will be ready in a minute. You ask him to wait.

   _____

Connections: Formal and Informal Short Answers

When family members or friends make requests, you can answer with informal short answers.

Request: "Can you give me a hand with this?"

Informal Short Answers

To answer yes:	To answer no:
Sure.	Sorry, I can't right now.
OK.	Sorry, ___(name)___, but I'm busy.
No problem.	Sorry, ___(name)___, I don't have time.

When a stranger or a person at work makes a formal request, you can answer with formal short answers.

Formal Short Answers

To answer yes:	To answer no:
Certainly.	I'm very sorry, but I can't right now.
Of course.	I'm afraid I can't.
I'd be happy to.	I'm so sorry, but I'm late.

When you say no to a request, you usually give a reason.

5 Write a short answer for each request. Then practice the conversations with a partner.

Example: Boss: Sandra, would you please mail this immediately?
Employee: Certainly. I'll be right there.

1. Boss: Would you make sure that those boxes get on the next truck?
   You: _____

2. Friend: Will you help me with this homework?
   You: _____

3. Co-worker: Can you lend me a hand over here?
   You: _____

4. Teacher: Would you please turn off the lights?
   You: _____

5. Roommate: Will you please get the door?
   You: _____

Two-Word Verbs

Hang up your jackets.

Tran and Lan **are hanging up** their jackets.

He **is looking up** the word in the dictionary.

Here are some two-word verbs you may already know:
- find out = learn information
- call up = phone
- look for = try to find
- turn up = make the volume louder
- turn down = make the volume softer

Two-word verbs have two parts—a verb and a preposition. The meaning of two-word verbs is usually different from the meaning of each word alone. Two-word verbs change forms to reflect person and tense.

6 Vitya has forgotten his homework assignment for next week. What should he do? Read his list of ideas to solve this problem.

1. First, look for the list of students' names.
2. Next, look up the phone numbers of some students in the phone book
3. Call up some of the students. (I hope they're home.)
4. Maybe they won't be home. Call back several times.
5. Talk to someone. Find out the assignment. (I hope.)

7 With a partner, form *wh*-questions and answers with *going to* for each of the points on Vitya's list.

Example: A: What is Vitya going to look for?
B: He's going to look for the list of students' names.

With a partner or a group, think of more things that Vitya can do to find what his homework assignment is. Use two-word verbs. Look at pages 170–171 if you need help. Write down your ideas and share them with the class.

Unit 5

Focus on Vocabulary

More Two-Word Verbs

Use the following two-word verbs to complete the sentences below.

clean up   take out   plug in   hang up   put on
drop off   take off

1. Rob should _____ the kitchen.

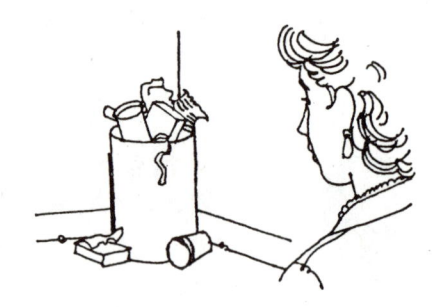

2. Joel should _____ the computer.

3. Malik should _____ his coat and gloves.

4. Ramziya should _____ the garbage.

5. Yolanda should _____ her coat.

6. The children should _____ some more clothing before they go out.

48   Unit 5

Two-Word Verbs (Separable and Inseparable)

Separable
Take off your coat. **Take** your coat **off**.
Hang up your coat. **Hang** your coat **up**.

take . . . off	put . . . on	turn . . . up
plug . . . in	hang . . . up	turn . . . down
find . . . out	clean . . . up	call . . . up

Inseparable
I'm **looking for** the phone book. Do you know where it is?
NOT *I'm looking the phone book for.

Many two-word verbs are separable. A noun can come between the two parts. Other two-word verbs, such as *look for*, are never separated.

> Put all endings on the verb, not on the preposition.

8 In a group, copy the nine separable two-word verbs above onto separate cards. Put the cards into a bag and then choose one. Write a sentence separating the parts of the verb. Then read your sentences to the class.

9 Work with a partner. Take turns making informal requests with each of these separable two-word verbs. Answer with appropriate short answers. Write your requests on the lines provided. Then practice the conversations.

Example: A: Can you *turn* the lights *on*?
B: No problem.

1. pick up _____
2. take off _____
3. hang up _____
4. look up _____
5. drop off _____
6. clean up _____

Unit 5   49

Two-Word Verbs with Pronouns

Take off your coat. Take **it** off.
Hang **it** up in the closet.

Your toys are all over the house.

Please pick **them** up.

Separable two-word verbs are often separated by pronouns. You can use a pronoun when you think the listener knows what you are talking about.

10 Work with a partner. Write the missing request in each conversation. Use the following two-word verbs with pronouns: *wake up, throw out, turn down, pick up, take out, hang up, turn off.* After you finish, practice the conversations.

Example: Father: The radio is too loud. Will you turn it down?
Son: OK, Dad.

1. Wife: Oh, no. There's the garbage truck across the street. We forgot to take the garbage out last night. _____
   _____?

   Husband: Right away.

2. Rosa: Mom, the refrigerator smells terrible. I think there's something rotten in there.
   Mom: Well, Rosa, open a few containers and find the spoiled food.
   Rosa: Mom! I found it!
   Mom: Good! _____?
   Rosa: Sure.

3. Mom: Kim, your room is a mess. There are so many clothes on the floor I can't even walk through your room. _____
   _____?

   Kim: OK, Mom. I'll do it as soon as I finish my homework.

Small Talk: Would you repeat that, please?

When you can't understand someone, it doesn't always mean that you don't understand English. Native speakers don't always understand, either. When you don't understand something, you can use the following phrases:

Excuse me?	Would you repeat that, please?
Pardon?	Could you repeat that, please?
What was that?	Could you say that again?

11 Work with a partner. Practice the conversations in Exercise 5 on page 46 again. Pretend that you can't understand the requests. Use the expressions in Small Talk above to say that you don't understand.

Partnerwork ▶ Person A

Work with a partner. Person A looks at this page. Person B looks at page 52 only. Imagine that you live together. You and your partner have to leave the house in two hours to catch a plane. You each have a list of chores. Decide together which chores to do and who will do them. (You don't have to do all the chores if you feel they aren't important.) You can use requests to ask your partner to do some of the chores on your list. Next to each chore, write the name of the person (A, B, or no one) who will do that chore.

1. Clean up the kitchen (30 minutes)
2. Call up Fred at work to tell him about schedule change (5 minutes)
3. Drop off Suzy at Grandma's (1 hour)
4. Drop off overdue books at the library (30 minutes)
5. Pick up the clothes in Suzy's room (10 minutes)
6. Hang up coats in the closet (2 minutes)
7. Call up the airline to see if the flight is on time (5 minutes)
8. Take out the garbage (5 minutes)
9. Look for the suitcases (5 minutes)
10. Pack (30 minutes)

Partnerwork
▶ Person B

Work with a partner. Person B looks at this page. Person A looks at page 51 only. Imagine that you live together. You and your partner have to leave the house in two hours to catch a plane. You each have a list of chores. Decide together which chores to do and who will do them. (You don't have to do all the chores if you feel they aren't important.) You can use requests to ask your partner to do some of the chores on your list. Next to each chore, write the name of the person (A, B, or no one) who will do that chore.

1. Clean up the bathroom (15 minutes)
2. Clean up my desk (10 minutes)
3. Drop off the cat at the neighbor's house (10 minutes)
4. Drop off the newspaper at the recycling center (10 minutes)
5. Call up the cab company and order a cab for 3:30 (2 minutes)
6. Unplug the computer (1 minute)
7. Call up a neighbor and ask her to water the plants (5 minutes)
8. Plug in the electric timer for the lights (1 minute)
9. Turn down the heat (1 minute)
10. Pack (30 minutes)

Use What You Know

Write about things you and your family did last week. Use as many two-word verbs as you can. Include one false statement. If you need help, look at pages 170-171. Read your list to the class. Your classmates will guess what you didn't really do.

Wrapping Up

Work with a partner. Pick six of the places listed below. Write a request and a short answer for each place. Decide together if you need a formal or informal request and answer. Then act out your conversations for the class. Your classmates will guess where your conversation takes place.

Example: *at home*
A: Can you answer the phone?
B: Sure.

at home	at the bank	at a restaurant	at a friend's house
at work	at a bus stop	at the post office	at a hospital
at school	at the airport	at a gas station	at the supermarket

- Polite Offers and Requests with *Would like*
- *Would rather/Would rather not*
- *One/Ones/Another one*
- Review of Singular and Plural Nouns

Unit 6   I'd like a cup of decaf, please

Where is Jean? Who has she met? Describe each scene.

Unit 6 53

Setting the Scene

Jean: Ana! What a surprise! Sit down and have a cup of coffee!
Waitress: Would you like something?
Ana: Yes. I'd like a cup of decaf, please.
Jean: By the way, would you like to go to a jazz club tonight with some friends and me?
Ana: Oh, I'd rather stay home tonight. I like jazz, but I'm a bit tired.

Polite Offers and Requests with *Would like*

Waitress: **Would** you **like** something?
Customer: Yes, **I'd like** a cup of coffee, please.
Waitress: What kind of coffee **would** you **like**? Regular or decaf?
Customer: Decaf, please.

You can use *would like* to make a polite request.
In responding to offers, you can contract *would* like this:

I **would** = I**'d**   You **would** = You**'d**
He **would** = He**'d**   We **would** = We**'d**
She **would** = She**'d** They **would** = They**'d**

> In conversation, use the contraction *'d*.

1 Listen to these people talk about things they like and things they'd like. Check the correct column for each sentence you hear.

	like	would like ('d like)
1.		
2.		
3.		
4.		
5.		
6.		

54   Unit 6

2 Work with a partner. Practice these conversations. Guess where these people are. Then talk about where these places are in your community.

Example: A: Would you like anything else?
B: Yes, I'd like a cup of decaf, please.

1. A: Good morning. I'd like to send this to Thailand.
   B: Is that first class?

2. A: Hello. I'd like to cash this.
   B: Yes ma'am. Would you like it all in twenties?

3. A: Next.
   B: I'd like two pounds of shrimp, please.
   A: Sure. Here you are.

4. A: I'd like to see some floor mats for an '89 Mustang.
   B: They're in the last aisle, toward the back of the store.

5. A: I'd like to know what the round-trip fare is from Los Angeles to Mexico City.
   B: Let me check the current fares in the computer.

6. A: I'd like to return this book.
   B: Right at the end of this counter.

7. A: My name is Jonathan Fried. I'd like to make an appointment for my son sometime next week.
   B: All right, Mr. Fried. How about Wednesday at 3:30?

8. A: I'd like to register my new car.
   B: Fill out all these forms, get in line again, and have your check or money order already filled out to the State Department of Transportation.

Unit 6   55

Would rather/Would rather not

A: Would you like to get something to eat? B: No, **I'd rather** eat here.

A: Would you like some coffee? B: No, **I'd rather not** have coffee this late at night. It keeps me up.

To express a preference, you can say *I would rather* or *I would rather not*.

A: How much money do you make?
B: **I'd rather not say.**

When someone asks you a question you don't want to answer, you can say *I'd rather not say*.

Use the contraction *I'd rather* in conversation.

3 Write answers to the following questions. Use *I'd rather* or *I'd rather not* in your answers. If you answer "I'd rather not," give a reason. Then take turns practicing the conversations with a partner.

Example: A: Would you like to go out to dinner tonight?
B: I'm so tired I'd rather stay home. How about tomorrow night?

A: How much did you pay for your house?
B: I'd rather not say.

1. Would you like some lemonade?

2. Would you like to go to the movies tonight?

3. Why did you get divorced?

4. Would you pick up a newspaper on your way home?

5. Do you want to go get some frozen yogurt?

6. Could you baby-sit for me tonight?

Connections: Agreeing and Disagreeing About Likes/Dislikes

Here are some ways to agree with someone who likes something:

A: I like decaf.   B: I do, too./So do I.

Here are some ways to express disagreement with someone who likes something:

A: I like decaf.   B: Really? I don't.
I don't care for it.

You can say: I like decaf. I like to drink decaf. I like drinking decaf.

Here are some ways to agree with someone who expresses a dislike:

A: I don't like eating dinner late.   B: I don't either./Neither do I.

Here are some ways to disagree with someone who expresses a dislike:

I don't like eating dinner late.   Really? I do.
I don't mind it.

---

4 **Work with a partner. Take turns telling each other what you like to do. Take turns agreeing or disagreeing with each other.**

Example: A: I like to eat spaghetti.
B: I do, too. I like talking about politics.
A: Really? I don't.

5 **Take turns telling each other what you don't like to do. Take turns agreeing or disagreeing with each other.**

Example: A: I don't like ironing.
B: I don't either. I don't like going to the dentist.
A: Really? I don't mind it.

6 **Walk around the classroom. Talk to classmates about things they like and don't like to do, eat, and drink. Agree or disagree with the people you talk to.**

Example: A: What do you like to do?
B: I like to go to art museums.
A: I do, too.
B: What don't you like to eat?
A: I don't like peas.
B: I don't either.

Focus on Vocabulary

Different Kinds of Clothing

Shoes

What kind of shoes would you like?

| sneakers |  loafers |  high heels |  wing tips |  pumps |  boots |

Shirts

What kind of shirt would you like?

| turtleneck |  T-shirt |  short-sleeved shirt | 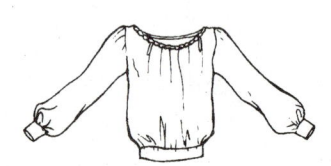 blouse |  dress shirt |

Jackets

What kind of jacket would you like?

| man's sport jacket |  woman's jacket |  windbreaker |  denim jacket |  bomber jacket |

7   Work with a partner. Role-play a conversation between a customer and a salesperson in a store. Choose an item from each of the three categories in the Focus on Vocabulary box. Role-play six conversations.

Example: Customer: I'd like some shoes.
Salesperson: What kind of shoes would you like?
Customer: I'd like some loafers.

58 Unit 6

One/Ones/Another one

I'd like to try on these shoes.
Which **ones**?
These sneakers.

I'd like to try on a jacket.
Which **one**?
That **one** over there.

How do you like the jacket?
I'm not sure. I'd like to try on **another one**.

8 Work with a partner. Practice these conversations. Then substitute the items with others from the Focus on Vocabulary box on page 58.

1. Customer: I'd like to return *these sneakers*.
   Salesperson: Why?
   Customer: They're too small.
   Salesperson: Would you like *some larger ones*?
   Customer: Yes, but I'd like a different color.
   Salesperson: What color would you like?
   Customer: Some _____ ones.

2. Customer: I'd like to return *this windbreaker*.
   Salesperson: Why?
   Customer: It's too small.
   Salesperson: Would you like *another one*?
   Customer: Yes, but I'd like a different color.
   Salesperson: What color would you like?
   Customer: A _____ one.

9 Complete these sentences with *one*, *ones*, or *another one*.

1. Jim has a new car, but he hasn't sold his old _____.

2. "Do you like the dress?" "It's all right, but I'd like to see _____."

3. These boots are made well, but the _____ I saw at the other shoe store are better-looking.

4. "Which _____ is your favorite?" "The _____ on the right."

Unit 6   59

Review of Singular and Plural Nouns

Singular (one)	**Plural (two or more)**
tree	trees
flower	flowers
bush	bushes
baby	babies
class	classes
tomato	tomatoes

Most nouns have a singular and plural form.

child	children
man	men
woman	women
tooth	teeth
foot	feet
mouse	mice

Some nouns have a special plural form.

> See Appendix page 169 for spelling rules.

10 Work with a partner. How many people and things are in the picture below? Take turns asking and answering questions about the number of people and things you see. Ask about as many people and things as you can.

    Example: A: How many *women* are there?
                 B: There *are two woman* in the picture.
                     How many _____ are there?
            A: _____

11 Now look at this picture. With your partner, find as many differences between this picture and the one on page 60 as you can. Write sentences about the differences on a separate sheet of paper. Compare your sentences with your classmates.

Example: *There's one _____ in this picture, but there are two _____ in the picture on page 60.*

In Your Own Words

Work in groups. Discuss your likes, dislikes, wants, and preferences. Practice agreeing and disagreeing with one another. Some topics you could discuss are food, sports, hobbies, music, movies, and TV programs.

Example: Helena: Well, of course, I love opera. It is the best music of all.
Gloria: Really? I don't care for opera. I like country-western music.
Sergio: I'd rather listen to classical music. It's so relaxing.
Gloria: But you can't dance to it. I'm learning how to line-dance. It's really fun.

Wrapping Up

Think about one thing you like, one thing you'd like to do, and one thing you'd rather be doing right now. Write each of these ideas on a separate piece of paper. Put all of the papers from the class into a bag.

Example: *I like watermelon. I'd like to win the lottery. I'd rather be sleeping.*

Each student will now choose three other pieces of paper from the bag. Walk around the room and ask questions to find the people who wrote the sentences you have.

Example: *Do you like watermelon?*
Would you like to win the lottery?
Would you rather be sleeping?

When someone answers yes, write his or her name on the back of that piece of paper. When you find all three people, write a sentence about each person on the lines below. Then tell the class what you learned about these three people.

1. _____
2. _____
3. _____

Review: Units 4–6

1. **Work in groups.** Think about things you have done, have never done, and have always wanted to do. Write two sentences about yourself that are true, and write one sentence about yourself that is false. Read your three sentences to your group. Then your classmates can try to guess which of the sentences about you is not true.

   Example: *I have been a salesclerk for six months.*
   I have never been a waiter.
   I have always wanted to have my own business.

2. Brainstorm a list of two-word verbs. Write them on the board. Divide into two teams. Each team takes turns acting out a verb without speaking. The other team guesses the verb. As verbs are guessed, cross them off the list on the board.

3. Read the following story. Circle the singular nouns and underline the plural nouns. On the lines below, write the singular forms of the plural nouns and the plural forms of the singular nouns.

   Jean and her sister Norma usually get together for lunch on Saturdays. Jean tells Norma about her students, and Norma tells Jean about her job.

   Norma works in a clothing store. She sells clothing for men, women, and children. She always has interesting stories about her customers. She told Jean this story:

   "On Friday afternoon, I was tired, and my feet hurt. At three o'clock, a woman came into the shoe department. First, she looked at sneakers. Then she tried some on. Next, she looked at high heels. She tried some of them on. Then she looked at boots, and she tried some of those on too.

   "At four o'clock, the woman started to leave. I said, 'Don't you want to buy any shoes?' The woman said, 'No. I have to see the dentist at four-thirty about a sore tooth. I was just looking.' I had to put away thirty pairs of shoes!"

   _____
   _____
   _____
   _____

4 Work with a partner. Look at the menu below. Practice the conversation. Then role-play a waiter and a customer. Change the foods and drinks in the conversation. Finally, create your own conversation and present it to the class.

Waiter: Would you like something to drink before dinner?
Customer: No, thanks. I'd rather wait.
(*Ten minutes later*)
Waiter: What would you like?
Customer: I'd like the *marinated chicken*.
Waiter: Would you like soup or a salad with that?
Customer: I'd like a salad, please.
Waiter: A *house salad*, *a garden salad*, or *a Caesar salad*?
Customer: *A garden salad*, please.
Waiter: What kind of dressing would you like—Italian, French, blue cheese, or garlic?
Customer: *Italian*, please.
Waiter: What would you like to drink?
Customer: I'd like a glass of *Chardonnay*.
Waiter: Would you like some *French Chardonnay* or *American Chardonnay*?
Customer: I'd rather have some *American Chardonnay*, please.

Tony's Bistro

Appetizers
Deep-fried mushrooms
Stuffed cabbage leaves
Chopped liver
Marinated salmon
Avocado *au diable*
Shrimp cocktail

Salads
House salad
Garden salad
Spinach salad
Chef salad
Waldorf salad
Caesar salad

Wine
Cabernet Sauvignon
American Chardonnay
French Chardonnay

Beer
You name it

In the Park

Entrees
Sirloin steak
Rack of lamb
Veal cutlet in
  wine sauce
Marinated chicken
Chicken tarragon
Poached trout
Sole meuniere
Baked sea bass
Batter-fried perch
Jumbo sea scallops

Soup
Chicken noodle soup
Beef soup
Spicy Cajun soup
Consommé

Desserts
Black Forest cake
Chocolate mousse
House apple pie
Baked Alaska

- Noncount Nouns
- Nouns with No Article
- Future with *Going to*

Unit 7   I'm going to make eggplant curry

Victor and Chan Ho are in an Asian market. What kinds of food can you buy here? Do you ever buy Asian food?

Setting the Scene

Victor: Could you give me some advice? I'm going to make eggplant curry.
Chan Ho: Oh, that's one of my favorite dishes. You need garlic, mustard seeds, curry powder, some onions, oil, rice, and a couple of eggplants.
Victor: I don't see any curry powder here.
Chan Ho: They have cans of curry powder right over there.

Noncount Nouns

Noncount nouns generally do not have a plural form. You cannot use *a*, *an*, or numbers in front of noncount nouns without changing the meaning. But you can use *some*.

I'd like **some meat**.	NOT *I'd like a meat.
I'd like **some advice**.	NOT *I'd like an advice.

> Use singular verbs with noncount noun subjects.

There are different categories of noncount nouns. Here are just some of them:

Liquids:	water	coffee	gasoline	shampoo
Solids:	meat	fruit	soap	jewelry
Nature words:	air	fog	rain	snow
Idea words:	beauty	peace	happiness	intelligence

1 Listen to your teacher. Write the nouns you hear in each sentence. Then work in a group. Decide together if each noun is count or noncount.

1. _____
2. _____
3. _____
4. _____
5. _____
6. _____
7. _____

2 Work in groups. Look at the four categories of noncount nouns in the grammar box on page 66. Think of more nouns for each category. Make a list.

3 Look at the recipe for Eggplant Curry at the bottom of the page. With a partner, take turns asking and answering questions about the ingredients in the recipe. Be careful to pronounce the *s* on the ends of words correctly. Remember that there are several ways to pronounce *s* on the ends of words. Sometimes *s* sounds like /s/, and sometimes it sounds like /z/.

Example: A: How much oil is in the recipe?
B: Two tablespoons.

B: How many eggplants are in the recipe?
A: Two large eggplants. OR Two large ones.

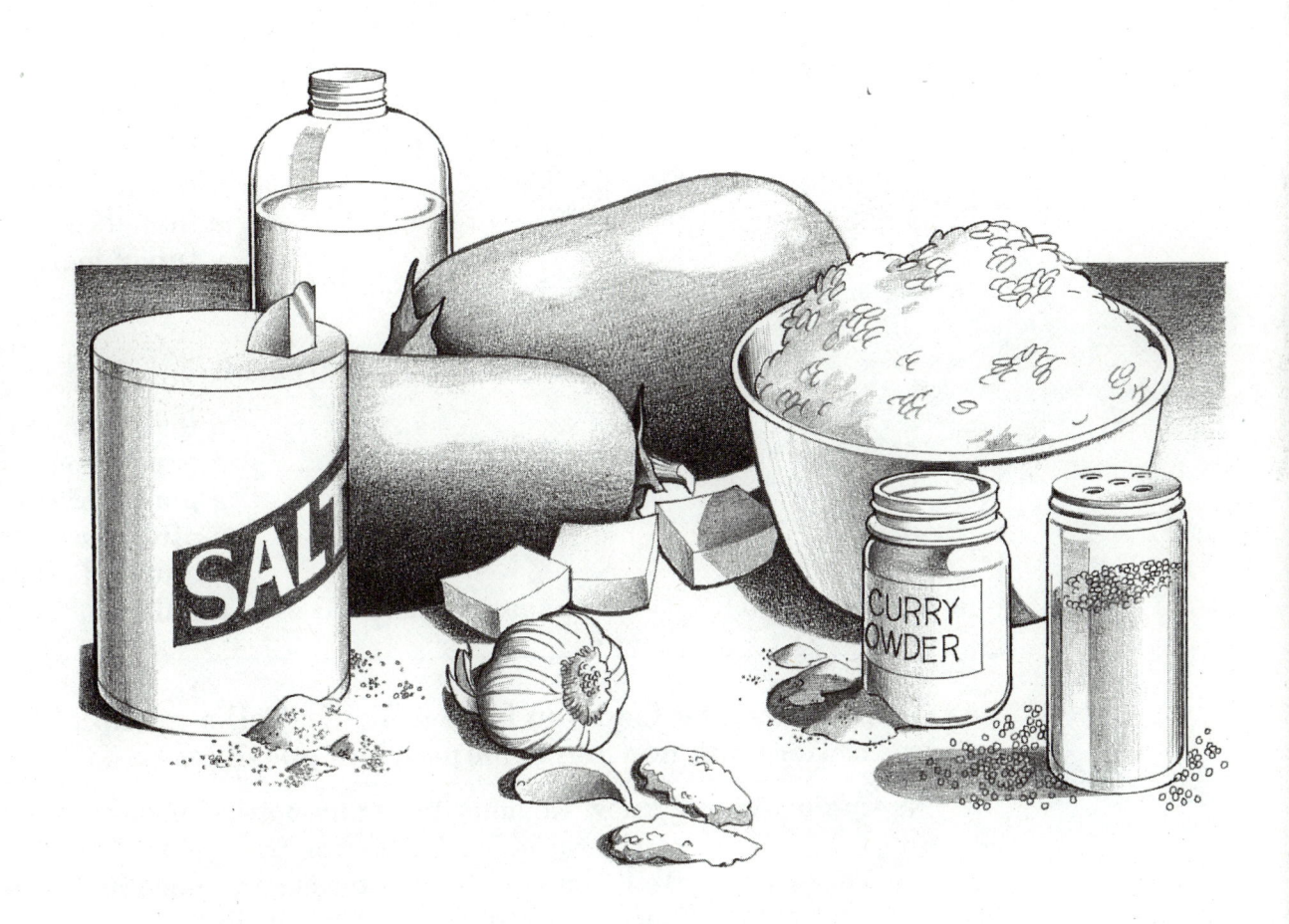

Recipe for Eggplant Curry

2 tablespoons of oil
1½ teaspoons of mustard seeds
1½ teaspoons of salt
2 teaspoons of curry powder
2 cloves of garlic (minced)
2 large eggplants (cut into cubes)
4 cups of cooked rice

Unit 7   67

Focus on Vocabulary

Quantifiers for Noncount Nouns

You can count noncount nouns if you use special words called quantifiers. There are quantifiers for food, packages, and measurement.

Quantifiers for Food

a **head** of cabbage

three **heads** of cabbage

a **bunch** of parsley
a **clove** of garlic
an **ear** of corn
a **stalk** of celery

Quantifiers for Packages

a **bag** of rice

three **bags** of rice

a **jar** of mustard
a **carton** of yogurt
a **can** of soup
a **bottle** of olive oil
a **box** of cereal
a **tub** of margarine
a **package** of spaghetti

Quantifiers for Measurement

a **teaspoon** of oil

three **teaspoons** of oil

a **teaspoon** of salt
a **cup** of flour
a **pound** of rice
a **pint** of sour cream
a **quart** of orange juice
a **gallon** of milk

4 Think about the food you have at home. Tell a group about it. Use quantifiers and noncount nouns when possible.

Example: A: I know we don't have any bottles of soda in our refrigerator. We have some fruit juice, I think.
B: Well, I'm sure we don't have any juice in our house. Nobody in my family likes it. But I have a package of tofu in the refrigerator for dinner tomorrow.

5 Work with a partner. Look at the grocery list below. Do you see anything wrong? There are five mistakes with the quantifiers in this list. Find and correct the mistakes. Then check your work with another pair of classmates.

2 ears of celery
1 jar of fish sauce
2 pints of shrimp
1 lb. of eggs
1 gallon of milk

1 jar of orange juice
2 heads of cabbage
1 bunch of noodles
2 boxes of cereal

6 Victor bought the ingredients for eggplant curry at the Asian market, but he isn't sure how to make the curry. When he got home, he called Chan Ho for the directions.

The following directions are not in the correct order. Listen to Chan Ho's directions. Number the directions in order from 1 to 7.

_____ Add the mustard seeds.

_____ Cook and stir for 5 minutes.

_____ When the seeds start to pop, add the salt, curry powder, garlic, and onion.

_____ Cook and stir for 15 minutes.

_____ Heat the oil in a large frying pan.

_____ Serve immediately over rice.

_____ Add the eggplant.

Unit 7

69

Nouns with No Article

Noncount Nouns: **Shrimp** is expensive.
I like **sugar** and **cream** in my coffee.

Plural Count Nouns: **Onions** are usually not expensive.
Do you cook with **chili peppers**?

Shrimp is expensive. (general)
The shrimp on the table was on sale. (specific)

Use *the* with noncount or plural count nouns only when you are talking about specific items.

Do not use *the* in general statements with noncount nouns and plural count nouns.

7 Work with a partner from a country other than yours, if possible. Compare the prices of the items below in your native countries. Discuss possible reasons for the differences.

Example: A: In Poland, computers and fax machines are very expensive. We import these things from Japan or the U.S.

B: In Japan, computers and fax machines are not too expensive. Many Japanese companies make computers and fax machines.

home computers	fax machines	education
video cameras	surgery	prescription drugs
homes	cars	gold jewelry
fresh fish	fresh fruit	medical care
weddings	funerals	furniture

8 Work in groups. Talk about habits that people from your native country think are bad for you. Discuss differences between your native countries and the U.S. After your discussion, tell the class something interesting you learned.

Example: A: In Vietnam and China, people think milk, cheese, and butter are very bad for your health. Americans don't think so.

B: Yes, that's true in Korea, too. We put fruit juice in our baby bottles, not milk.

C: In my country, almost all men smoke. No one thinks cigarettes are bad for you. But here everyone is afraid of cancer. Most Americans don't smoke.

9 Look at the objects below. On a separate sheet of paper, write sentences about all of these items. Use the adjectives listed below or think of other adjectives. Many different sentences are possible.

Example: *Sugar is sweet.*

delicious	healthy	expensive	fattening	beautiful
sweet	flammable	unhealthy	dirty	spicy
important	useful	tasteless	wonderful	cheap

1. shrimp
2. fish
3. tomato paste
4. sugar
5. money
6. soda
7. pepper
8. gasoline
9. soap
10. jewelry
11. coffee
12. meat

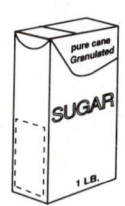

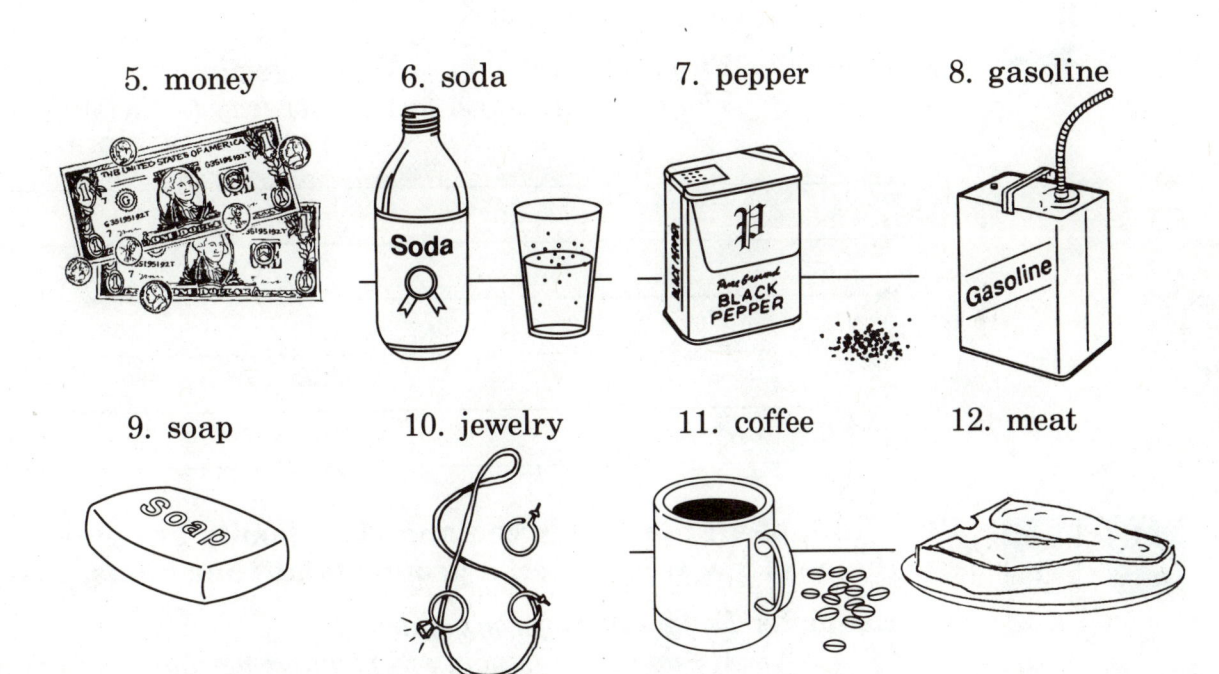

10 Now work with a partner. Ask your partner yes/no questions about all of your sentences. Your partner will agree or disagree. If your partner thinks your sentence is not correct, he or she will tell you.

Example: A: Is soap expensive?
B: No, soap isn't expensive. It's cheap.

Make a list of your disagreements and report them to the class. Listen to what other students say about your ideas.

Unit 7

Future with *Going to*

Sergio and Thuy **are going to have** dinner at Victor's.
Sergio **is going to make** a Chinese meal.

Is Sergio **going to help** Victor cook?
Who **is going to be** there?
When **are** they **going to get** together?

You can use *be* + *going to* + verb to talk about something you plan to do in the future.

> When speaking we often say "gonna" for *going to*.

11 With a partner, think of some things that could happen to Victor, Thuy, Sergio, and Chan Ho before, during, or after Victor's dinner. Use *going to*. Write your ideas below. Then read one of your sentences to the class.

Example: *Victor is going to burn the whole dinner.*
Thuy is going to get lost on her way to Victor's house.

1. _____
2. _____
3. _____
4. _____
5. _____
6. _____

12 Think of all the things you and your family are planning to do in the next few weeks. Tell a group about your plans. Use *going to*.

Example: *I'm going to get my hair cut.*
My daughter is going to pick out her quinceañera dress.
We are going to visit our relatives for Sunday dinner.

Small Talk: Talking About the Weekend

In the United States, people talk about the weekend a lot. On Friday, they often say, "Have a nice weekend!" or "What are you going to do this weekend?" Here are some ways to respond:

Have a nice weekend!	Thanks. You, too.
Have a good weekend!	I will. Thanks.
	You, too. See you Monday.
What are you going to do this weekend?	Not much. What are you going to do?
	Nothing special. What about you?
	I'm going out.

13 Walk around the classroom. Practice talking about the weekend with your classmates and teacher. Take turns asking and answering questions. Use the Small Talk sentences as models.

Example: A: What are you going to do this weekend?
B: I'm going to get my hair cut. What about you?

Partnerwork ▶ Person A

Person A looks at this page only. Person B looks at page 74 only. Your picture and your partner's picture are not exactly the same. Take turns asking and answering questions about your pictures to find what is different. Find eight differences in the pictures.

Example: A: Do you have three tomatoes?
B: No. I don't have any tomatoes.

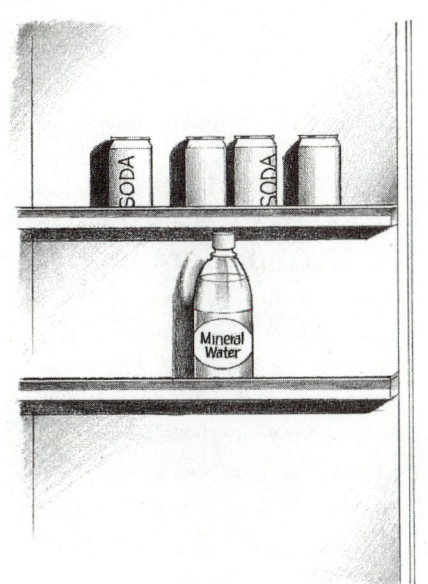

Unit 7 73

Partnerwork ▶ Person B

Person B looks at this page only. Person A looks at page 73 only. Your picture and your partner's picture are not exactly the same. Take turns asking and answering questions about your pictures to find what is different. Find eight differences in the pictures.

Example: B: Do you have one carton of eggs?
A: No. I don't have any eggs.

Use What You Know

What is your favorite recipe? Write the ingredients on a piece of paper. Use quantifiers when possible. Then read the ingredients to the class. The class will try to guess what the recipe is for.

Wrapping Up

Imagine that some of your friends or relatives are planning to move to the United States. Write a letter to prepare them for the changes they are going to find. Here is Victor's letter to his cousins, Pedro and Yolanda.

> Dear Yolanda and Pedro,
> I am so happy that you are both going to come to this country to live. But this country is very different from Mexico. You are probably going to think that Americans are not very warm. They don't like to hug and touch as much as we do. Also, you are both going to have to look hard for work! But I hope you will like it here. I do. See you soon!
> Love,
> Victor

> ♦ Direct and Indirect Objects
> ♦ Indirect Object Pronouns
> ♦ Verbs with *To* and *For*
> ♦ *Too* + Adjective
> ♦ *So* and *Because*

Unit 8 We gave her a big cake

What are Jean and her students doing? What are they celebrating? How do you know?

Setting the Scene

Gloria: Sergio, you missed Jean's party.
Sergio: I know. How was it?
Gloria: Great! We gave her a big cake.
Sergio: Where did you get it?
Gloria: Helena made it for her. I brought my camera, so I took a lot of pictures. But I hope it wasn't too dark. I couldn't use my flash because it was broken.
Sergio: I hope the pictures turn out.

Direct and Indirect Objects

The students	got	**a big cake**	**for Jean.**
(subject)	(verb)	(direct object)	(indirect object)

The direct object answers the question *What?*
What did the students get for Jean?

    The students got *a big cake* for Jean.
    Yoshiko gave *flowers* to Jean.

The indirect object answers the question
For what person? or To what person?
Who did the students have a party for?

    The students got a big cake *for Jean.*
    Yoshiko gave flowers *to Jean.*

> You can say *The students bought* **a big cake for Jean.** OR *The students* **bought Jean a big cake.**

1 Listen to your teacher read the following sentences. For each one, fill in the chart with the direct object (what) and the indirect object (for what person).

	Direct Object	**Indirect Object**
1.	_____	_____
2.	_____	_____
3.	_____	_____
4.	_____	_____
5.	_____	_____

2. Read these sentences. Underline the direct objects. Circle the indirect objects.

Example: *The students got a big cake for Jean.*

1. They bought candles for Jean.
2. Amir made a card for the teacher.
3. Yoshiko gave flowers to Jean.

Now put the indirect object before the direct object.

Example: *Helena made Jean a cake.*

3. Here are some gifts a family gave each other for Christmas. In a group, talk about the gifts people gave.

Example: *Daryl gave Maggie a book. Maggie gave a sweater to her father.*

4. Finish these sentences. Then compare your answers with a partner. There are many possible correct answers.

Example: *Chan Ho gave his wife a gold watch for their anniversary.*

1. The students gave _____ a surprise party.
2. Gloria showed _____ the pictures of the party.
3. Gloria gave _____ a sweater.
4. Rosa brought _____ some books.

Indirect Object Pronouns

A: What did Tan give Jean?
B: He gave **her** a book about photography.

He gave | me / you / him / her / us / them | a book.

An indirect object pronoun can also go before a direct object. An indirect object pronoun replaces a noun.

5 What have you and your friends or family members given each other recently? Write sentences using indirect object pronouns. Then share your sentences with a group.

Example: *My mother gave me some money.*
I gave her a pretty scarf.

6 What are some of the gifts you have received in the last few years? In a group, write the ones you remember on the lines below. Tell your group about one of the most interesting gifts. Be sure to tell them what the occasion was, too.

Example: *My husband gave me a dozen red roses for our anniversary.*

1. _____
2. _____
3. _____
4. _____

7 Here are some occasions when people give presents in the U.S. On what occasions do you give presents? With a partner, talk about what you usually give on these or other occasions and the people you give presents to.

birthdays   Christmas   Mother's Day

weddings   Hanukkah   Father's Day

Example: *On my wedding anniversary, I usually give my husband/wife a _____.*
On _____, I give _____ a _____.

Verbs with *To* and *For*

A: Who did you **lend** your camera **to**?
B: I **lent** it **to** Gloria.

A: Who **are** you **making** that card **for**?
B: **I'm making** it **for** my ESL teacher.

Many verbs are followed by *to* or *for* plus an indirect object.

Use *to* with these verbs: give   Use *for* with these verbs: make
                             hand   buy
                             lend   get
                                                                     find

8 Listen to the conversations. Write the answers to the questions on the lines below. Read the example first.

Example: Chan Ho   bought a gold watch   for his wife

Who did something?	What did he/she do?	To or for which person?
1. _____	_____	_____
2. _____	_____	_____
3. _____	_____	_____
4. _____	_____	_____

9 Work with a partner. Take turns reading the sentences aloud to each other. Complete each sentence with *to* or *for*. Write your answers on the lines.

1. Helena made some Polish dumplings _____ everyone at the party.
2. Chan Ho found some beautiful earrings _____ Jean.
3. The other teacher lent her tape player _____ Jean's students.
4. Tan found a book about photography _____ Jean.
5. Yoshiko handed a piece of cake _____ Victor.
6. Amir gave a gold watch _____ his brother.
7. Gloria gave a hug _____ all the people who helped clean up.
8. Sergio made a big birthday card _____ Jean.

Focus on Vocabulary

Household Objects

Here are some things you might have at home or need to buy.

Kitchen Items

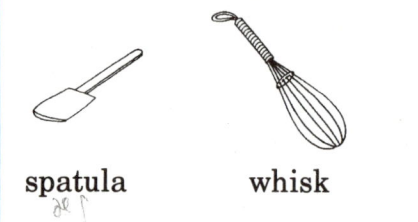

spatula whisk frying pan  stock pot  saucepan

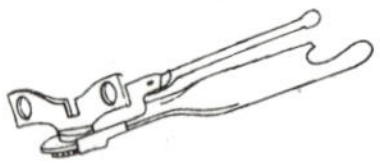

can opener  grater  strainer  roasting pan  salad bowl

Cleaning Items

dustpan broom 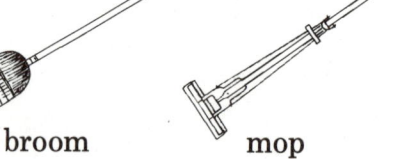 mop bucket  sponge

laundry basket  detergent dishwashing liquid window cleaner  squeegee

Tools

hammer  wrench screwdriver  pliers 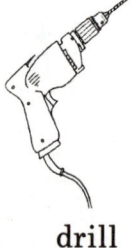 drill

10 Look at the pictures above. Which of these items do you have at home? Put a check next to each item you have. Then imagine that you have to borrow the objects you don't have from your neighbor. With a partner, take turns asking and answering questions about the items you want to borrow.

Example   A: Could you lend me a *spatula*?
               B: Sure, here you are. OR Sorry, I don't have one.

Too + Adjective

This tea is **too hot**. (I can't drink it.)

These shoes are **too small**. (I can't wear them.)

It's **too expensive**. (I can't buy it.)

11 Look at the pictures. For each picture, write a sentence on the lines below. Use *too* + adjective to explain the problem. There are many possible answers.

1.
2.
3.
4.
5.
6.

1. _____
2. _____
3. _____
4. _____
5. _____
6. _____

Unit 8   81

So and *Because*

Cause	Effect
Sergio had to work late,	**so** he missed Jean's party.
These shoes hurt my feet,	**so** I can't wear them.

Effect	Cause
Sergio missed Jean's party	**because** he had to work late.
We can't go to work	**because** the roads are all closed.

12 **Rewrite the sentences using *because*. Make any other necessary changes. Check your answers with a partner.**

Example: *Tan and Victor had to buy a present, so they were late for the party.*
Tan and Victor were late for the party because they had to buy a present.

1. Helena's new dress had a stain on it, so she took it back.

2. Yoshiko needed to pick up her children from the baby-sitter, so she left the party early.

3. Gloria wanted to take some pictures, so she brought her camera to the party.

13 **Rewrite the sentences below using *so*. Make any other necessary changes. Check your answers with a partner.**

Example: *Jean stopped dancing because she was thirsty.*
Jean was thirsty, so she stopped dancing.

1. Victor's little brother was very happy because he got a lot of presents for Christmas.

2. Sergio was upset because he had to work the night of Jean's party.

14 Think of three changes you want to make in your life. Then tell a group why you want to make each change. Use *so* or *because*.

Examples:
I want to change to the day shift because I don't like working at night.
I want to get a two-bedroom apartment because my apartment is too small.
I miss my family, so I want to go back to my country.

Connections: Returning Purchases

In the United States, people sometimes return things to stores. People return things that have a problem or don't work, that they don't like, or that don't fit.

Gloria gave her sister Rosa some jeans for her birthday, but they were too tight. Rosa is returning the jeans to the store where Gloria bought them.

Rosa:	I'd like to return these jeans.
Clerk:	Do you have a receipt?
Rosa:	No, they were a gift.
Clerk:	What's wrong with them?
Rosa:	They're too tight.
Clerk:	Would you like to exchange them for a larger size?
Rosa:	Yes.

15 Work with a partner. Practice the conversations. Take turns role-playing customer and clerk. Then act out one of the conversations for the class.

1. coat—too big
2. T-shirt—too tight
3. shorts—don't like them
4. shoes—hurt my toes
5. earrings—too heavy

Have you ever returned something to a store? Tell the class about it.

Use What You Know

Work with a partner. You each need six cards. On three of the cards, write the names of people you gave gifts to last year.

Example: /my son/   /my husband/   /my father/

On the three other cards, write three gifts you gave to other people last year. Use adjectives to describe the nouns. Do not include gifts you gave to the people named on your first three cards.

Example: /long-stemmed roses/   /a white cotton sweater/   /a homemade birthday cake/

Now turn the cards over. Student A will pick one of Student B's cards. Student A will ask Student B questions.

Example: Card: my son
           A: What did you give *your son*?
           B: I gave him a *T-shirt*.

           Card: a white cotton sweater
           A: Who did you give *a white cotton sweater* to?
           B: I gave it to *my mother*.

Wrapping Up

Sergio had a bad day yesterday. He wrote about it in his journal. Read what happened.

> Thursday
> I had a terrible day today. I forgot to set my alarm last night, so I overslept. Then my truck didn't start because the battery was dead. I was two hours late for work, so my boss was angry with me. Then the night clerk called in sick, so my boss asked me to work overtime. I missed Jean's birthday party because I had to work until midnight.

Write about a bad day or a good day you remember. Tell why the day was good or bad. Then share your story with a group or with the class.

_____
_____
_____
_____

84   Unit 8

> ♦ Modals of Necessity
> ♦ *Would like* + Infinitive
> ♦ Present Perfect Continuous

Unit 9 I've got to find a job fast

Class has just ended. Tan wants to talk to Jean about a problem. What do you think the problem is?

Unit 9   85

Setting the Scene

Tan: Jean, I'd like to talk to you. I lost my job! Now I've got to find another one.
Jean: Have you been looking for a new job?
Tan: No, I haven't. What should I do?
Jean: You could go to the Employment Office. I know someone there. Would you like to meet him?
Tan: Sure, but would you go with me? I haven't been studying English for very long.

Modals of Necessity

I/We/You/They **have to** work on Thursday.
He/She **has to** work on Thursday.

My car payment is due. I**'ve got to** get to the bank before it closes!

You look very sick. You**'d better** see a doctor.

You can use *have to* and *have got to* to talk about things that are necessary.
Have got to can be stronger than *have to*.
You can use *had better* to indicate urgent advice.

I **don't have to** work overtime this weekend.

You **must not** play in the street. (parent to child)

You can use *don't have to* to talk about things that are not necessary. You can use *must not* to talk about things that are forbidden or very strongly advised against.

1. Work with a group. Imagine that you lost your job yesterday. Think of things you have to do and things you don't have to do. Write your ideas and tell the class.

   Example: *I have to find another job. I have to write a résumé. I don't have to get up early tomorrow.*

86 Unit 9

2 Work with a partner. Look at the pictures below. Talk about the things Jean needs to do today and explain why. Write your sentences on a separate sheet of paper. Use *has to* or *has got to*.

Example: *Jean has to get gas today because her tank is almost empty.*

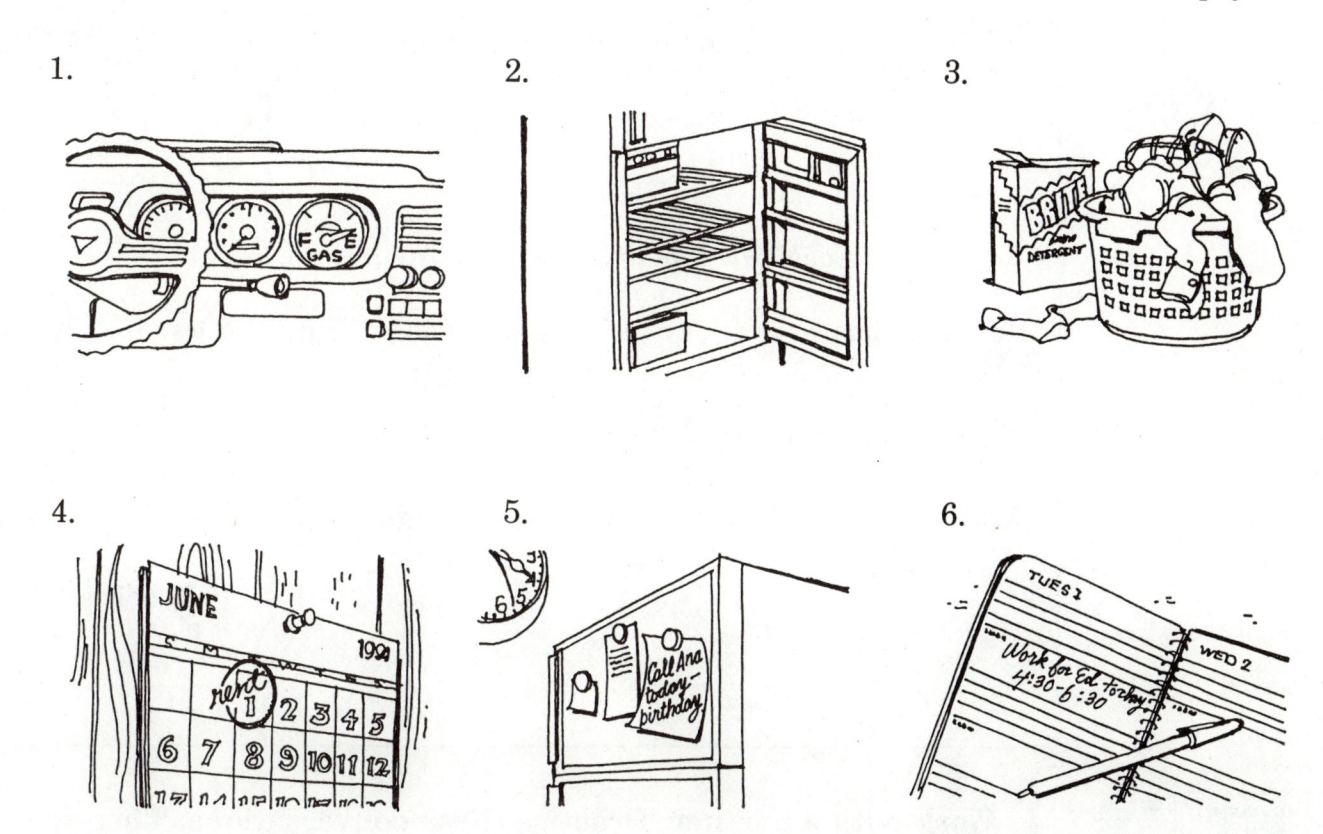

1.

2.

3.

4.

5.

6.

3 What are some things you have to do this week? Write them on a separate piece of paper. Use *have to* and *have got to*. Try to think of at least five things. Use the pictures in Exercise 2 for ideas. Then share your ideas with a group. What is the most interesting or important thing each person has to do this week? Decide together. Then tell the class one thing each person has to do this week.

Unit 9

87

Would like + Infinitive

Would you **like to** go out for coffee sometime?

Would | you
he
she
they
we | **like to** go?

> People often give a reason when they say no to an invitation.

You can use *would you like to . . .* to make invitations.

Here are some ways to say yes to invitations: Sure./I'd love to./That'd be great.

Here are some ways to say no to invitations:

Would you like to go to a party Saturday night?   I'd like to, but I have to work.
I'd love to, but I already have plans.
I wish I could. I have to baby-sit.

4 Work with a partner. Practice these conversations. Then try to create some similar conversations of your own. Perform one for the class.

A: Would you like to have a piece of cake? I made it last night.
B: Oh, yes. It looks fantastic.

A: Would you like to go see a movie this weekend?
B: I'd like to, but I'm working all weekend. How about next weekend?
A: That'd be great.

A: Would you like to have lunch at the new Indian restaurant today?
B: I'd love to. What time?
A: How about 12:30?
B: I'll be there.

5 Work with a partner. Take turns making and responding to invitations. Use the ideas below or make up your own.

1. Invite your classmate to your house for dinner.
2. Invite your classmate to go to a dance with you this weekend.
3. Invite your classmate to have a cup of coffee with you after class.
4. Invite your teacher to your daughter's birthday party.
5. Invite your teacher to a traditional New Year's celebration.

Small Talk: General Invitations

People in the United States often make general invitations to be polite. These invitations are a friendly way to end a conversation. They are not usually serious invitations.

A: Let's have lunch sometime.
B: I'd like that.
A: Good! Take care.
B: You too. Bye.

In the conversation above, neither person has talked about a specific time or place for lunch. The invitation is just friendly "small talk." People in the United States might invite you to their house, to go out to a restaurant, or to visit them at work. But unless they mention a specific time or place, they are not making a serious invitation.

6 Work with a partner. Take turns making and responding to general invitations. Use the ideas from Exercise 5 or make up your own.

7 Listen to your teacher. Mark whether the invitation you hear is a general invitation or a specific invitation (an invitation for a specific time and place).

General	Specific
1. _____	_____
2. _____	_____
3. _____	_____
4. _____	_____

Present Perfect Continuous

Jean: **Have you been looking** for a job?
Tan: No, I haven't.

I **haven't been studying** English for very long.
I **'ve been living** here for six months.

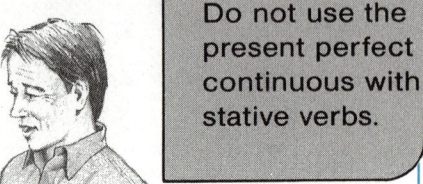

> Do not use the present perfect continuous with stative verbs.

| I | **'ve been studying** for days. | My car / It | **'s been making** noises all day. |

| I / You / We / They | **'ve been reading** all day. | He / She | **'s been reading** all day. |

You can use the present perfect continuous to talk about unfinished actions begun in the past and continued in the present. You can also use it for repeated actions begun in the past and continued in the present.

8 Dagmar is at a job interview. Practice this conversation.

Manager: How long have you been living in the U.S.?
Dagmar: For about two years.
Manager: Your English is very good. How long have you been studying?
Dagmar: Oh, about five years.
Manager: I see. Tell me about what you've been doing here in New York.
Dagmar: For the last five months, I've been working as a salesperson in a department store. But I've got to find another job.
Manager: Oh? Why? Is there something wrong with your job?
Dagmar: Yes. I have to stand all day. I've been having a lot of trouble with my feet.
Manager: I see. You should look for another job. Tell me more about what you've been doing.
Dagmar: I've been taking computer classes at night school since January.
Manager: Good. We need someone with computer skills.

9 Now, with a partner, role-play a job interview like the one in Exercise 8. Make up your own situation. Then perform it for the class.

10 Work with a partner. Look at this picture. What have these people been doing all day? Take turns asking and answering questions.

Angela
seal envelopes

Sergio
stamp envelopes

Rennie
put leaflets into envelopes

Enrique
put leaflets together

11 In a group, think of jobs you know about. Brainstorm a list of tasks that people have to do for these jobs and write them on a piece of paper. Next, imagine that you are at one of these jobs now. It's the end of a long day of work. Tell your group what you have been doing all day. Tell the class.

12 Complete the following sentences with the correct form of the present perfect continuous.

1. Maria (*study*) _____ all day, and now she's very tired. But she's ready for the test.

2. Tran and Lan (*walk*) _____ for an hour, but they still haven't found the shopping center.

3. Minh and I (*watch*) _____ a boring TV movie for a half hour. We're going to turn it off.

4. Yoshiko and Helena (*work*) _____ since 9:00 this morning. They're tired.

5. Reza (*wash*) _____ the dishes since we finished dinner, and Hushi (*dry*) _____ them.

6. Ernesto (*type*) _____ a résumé for the last three hours.

13 On a separate sheet of paper, write about three activities that you have been doing since you were young. (This means you still do these things now.) Then ask a partner if he or she has been doing those things as often in the U.S. as before.

Example: *I've been playing soccer since I was a child.*
I've been going to the movies since I was a child.
I've been playing cards since I was a child.

A: Have you been playing soccer as much in the U.S. as before?
B: Yes, I have. OR No, I haven't.

Focus on Vocabulary

Reduced Forms

People often say "*hafta*," "*hasta*," "*better*," and "*gotta*."

I have to work overtime tomorrow.	I "**hafta**" work overtime tomorrow.
Jean has to work for Ed on Thursday.	Jean "**hasta**" work for Ed on Thursday.
I've got to go.	I've "**gotta**" go. OR I gotta go.
You'd better not do that again.	You "**better**" not do that again.

People only use "*hafta*," "*hasta*," "*gotta*," and "*better*" in informal conversation, not in writing.

14 Listen to the sentences and write them on the lines below. Remember! Do not write "*hafta*," "*hasta*," or "*gotta*."

1. _____
2. _____
3. _____
4. _____
5. _____
6. _____

Connections: Ending a Conversation

When people want to end a conversation, they often use the words "OK" or "Well" followed by a pause. This tells the other person "I'm finished talking." People sometimes repeat "OK" or "Well" several times at the end of a conversation.

A: Well, it's been great talking to you.
B: Yeah, for me, too. Well, I guess I'll see you sometime.
A: Yeah. I'll see you soon.
B: OK. Take care.
A: OK. Talk to you soon.

Here are some expressions you can use to end conversations when you talk to friends, family, and co-workers.

I'll see you later.	OR	See you later.
I'll see you tomorrow.	OR	See you tomorrow.
I'll see you Monday.	OR	See you Monday.
I'll call you later.	OR	Call you later.
I'll talk to you later.	OR	Talk to you later.

Have a good day.
Have a nice evening.
Have a good weekend.
I've really got to go.

You can use these expressions in person and on the telephone. Try to use the expressions above to end your conversations.

15 Work with a partner. Practice this conversation. Then write another on your own. Share your conversation with a small group or the class.

A: Would you like to come over for dinner tonight?
B: I'd love to, but I have to baby-sit my nieces and nephews.
A: Well, how about tomorrow night?
B: That'd be great.
A: OK. So, I'll see you about seven.
B: OK. See you tomorrow then.
A: Great. Take care.
B: You too. Bye.

Use What You Know

Work with a partner. Write out a conversation between two friends. Include a greeting, an invitation (general or specific), and an ending. Practice your conversation and perform it for the class.

Wrapping Up

Read each of the situations below. What would each person say? Write sentences on the lines below each situation. There's more than one correct answer. Use the Modals of Necessity box on page 86 if you need help.

Example: A mother is angry because her daughter's room is a mess. She tells her daughter:
You've got to clean up that room today!

1. An older woman is worried about her friend. She thinks her friend should stop driving because her eyesight is not very good anymore. She tells her friend:
   _____

2. A wife is angry because her husband forgot to pay the gas bill. It was due ten days ago. She tells her husband:
   _____

3. A man thinks his wife needs to get a checkup because she hasn't had a checkup for ten years. He tells her:
   _____

4. The salespeople at a car dealership must sell more cars this month. The president of the company shouts:
   _____

5. A soccer coach wants his team to win more games. He tells them:
   _____

Review: Units 7–9

1. Sit in a large circle if possible. The class is going to make up a grocery list in alphabetical order. Practice using quantifiers for packages (see page 68). If no quantifier is possible, use *a* or *some* with your item. As each person adds an item to the list, he or she must repeat all the items that already have been said. The last person has to repeat the whole list to the rest of the class.

   Example: *I need* a bag of apples.
   I need a bag of apples and a loaf of bread.
   I need a bag of apples, a loaf of bread, and a bag of carrots.

2. Work in groups. Read each of the general statements below. Do you agree or disagree with each of these sentences? Tell why.

   1. Handguns are dangerous and should be illegal.
   2. Intelligence is more important than beauty.
   3. Marriage is necessary for happiness.
   4. Foreign cars are better than American cars.
   5. High school students should not have jobs.

   Now think of two more general statements your group agrees with. Write them on the lines below. Then share them with the class.

   1. _____
   2. _____

3. Every New Year, many Americans make resolutions, or promises, to be better people. On a separate sheet of paper, write two or three resolutions for yourself. Put all the resolutions in a bag. As a class, take turns picking resolutions, reading them aloud, and guessing who wrote them.

   Example: *I'm going to quit smoking.*
   I'm going to exercise every day.
   I'm going to speak English for one hour every day.

4 Think of things in your life that are difficult. Write them down using *too* + adjective. In groups, take turns talking about these situations. Explain why each situation is difficult.

Example: *My rent is too high. After food and the rent, there's nothing left. I want to save some money every month for a down payment on a house.*

5 Finish these sentences. Write about yourself. Then share your sentences with a small group or with the class.

1. I am studying English because _____
_____,
so I came to the United States.

2. I like _____, because
_____.

3. I don't like _____, so
_____

6 Imagine that today is a special holiday and you are going to give each of your classmates a present. You can buy or make something for each person. Look at the list of possible gifts below and add your own ideas. On a separate sheet of paper, write sentences about the things you are going to give to your classmates. Read your sentences to the class.

Example: *I'm going to make a card for Jorge.*
I'm going to buy a book for Hanh.
I'm going to give Yad a candle.

a book	a candle	a spice rack	a plant
a card	a clock	a T-shirt	a cup
a handbag	a book bag	a bouquet of flowers	a teapot

Add your gift ideas here:

_____
_____
_____

♦ Commands with *You*
♦ Inseparable Two-Word Verbs

Unit 10 I'm glad I ran into you

Yoshiko, her daughter, Keiko, and Tan are at the zoo. Did they come to the zoo together or did they meet by accident?

Setting the Scene

Yoshiko: What a surprise! I'm glad I ran into you. We're looking for the giraffes. Where are they?

Tan: I'm not sure. Let's ask someone. Excuse me. Could you tell me how to find the giraffes?

Guard: Sure. You go around the fountain until you come to the elephants. Then you turn left and go past the elephants. Turn right at the next walkway and you'll see the giraffes.

Tan: Thanks a lot. OK, Yoshiko, I think I can find the giraffes now.

Commands with *You*

First, **you go** around the fountain until you come to the elephants.

OR

First, **go** around the fountain until you come to the elephants.

Then, **you turn** left.   OR   Then, **turn** left.

You can use commands to give directions.

> You can use commands with or without *you*.

1 Listen to the directions. Do you hear a command with *you* or a command without *you*? Check the correct column for each sentence.

	With *You*	Without *You*
1.	_____	_____
2.	_____	_____
3.	_____	_____
4.	_____	_____
5.	_____	_____
6.	_____	_____

2   Look at the zoo map. Listen to the directions from the bears to the giraffes. Trace the route on the map with a pencil.

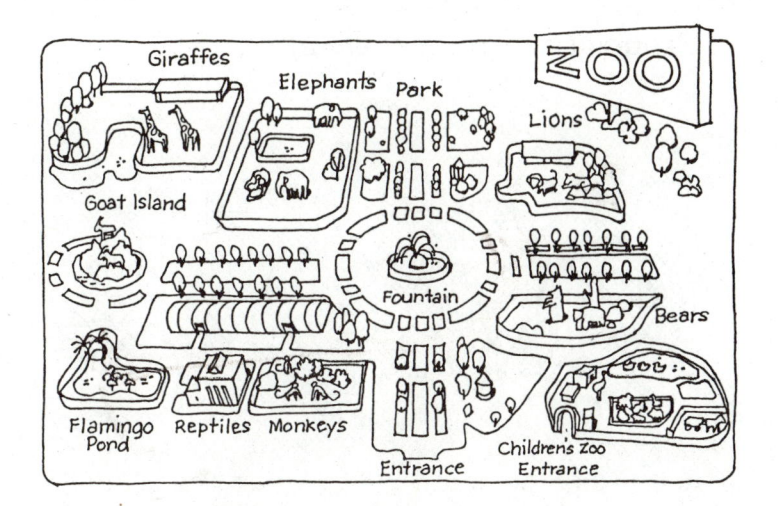

3   With a partner, compare the routes you drew above. Then take turns giving the directions.

Example: *First I went around the fountain. Then I walked until I came to the elephants.*

4   Work with a partner. Look at the map below and practice the conversation. Then trace the route on the map.

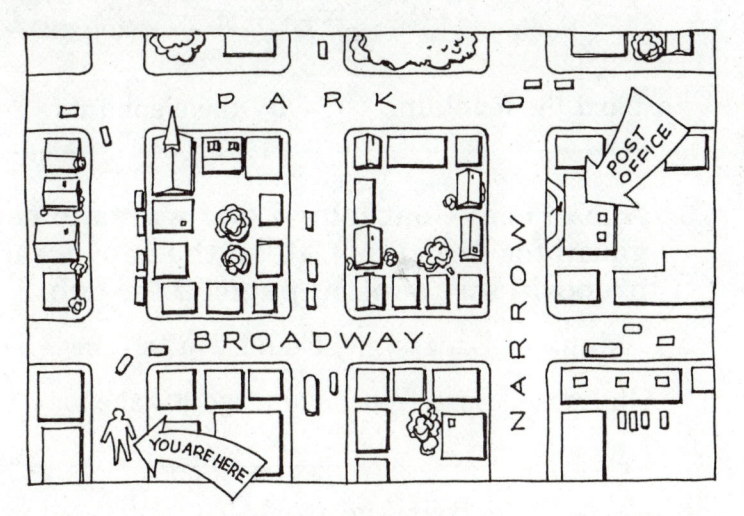

A: Excuse me. Could you tell me how to get to the post office?
B: Sure. Go down this street and turn right at the corner. You'll be on Broadway.
A: Yes.
B: Go down Broadway for two blocks. You'll come to the corner of Broadway and Narrow Street. Turn left on Narrow Street. The post office is on the right, about half a block from the corner.
A: Thanks a lot.

Focus on Vocabulary

Prepositions of Movement

around the fountain

past the bears

through the zoo

toward the fountain

by the elephants

across the patio

5 A man is at Goat Island and wants to see the lions. He asks a guard for directions. Read the conversation. Write the correct prepositions. Look at page 99 for help.

Man: Excuse me. Could you tell me where the lions are?

Guard: Sure. You have to go all the way _____ the zoo. First, go _____ the fountain. Then you turn left and go _____ the elephants. Turn right and go all the way _____ the park and you'll see the lions.

6 Now, find the places in Exercise 5 on the zoo map on page 99. With a pencil, trace the route the guard suggests. Compare routes with a partner.

Small Talk: Repeating Directions

When someone gives you directions, it's often hard to remember them. It helps to repeat them. Then you can check to see if you understood the directions.

Tan: Now, let's see. We're in front of the bears, so that means the giraffes are over on the other side of the zoo. OK. First, we go around the fountain until we come to the elephants. Then we turn left and go past the elephants. Turn right at the next walkway and we'll see the giraffes.

Yoshiko: So, let me see if I've got it right. First, we go around the fountain until we come to the elephants. Then we turn left and go past the elephants. We turn right at the next walkway and we're there.

Tan: Exactly!

7 Work with a partner. Using the map on page 99, take turns asking for and giving directions to the places listed below. Repeat the directions to make sure you understand. Use the conversation in Small Talk as a model.

You are at:	You want to go to:
1. the Children's Zoo entrance	the monkeys
2. the zoo entrance	the lions
3. the giraffes	the Children's Zoo
4. the fountain	Goat Island
5. the elephants	the Flamingo Pond
6. the lions	the reptiles

Unit 10

Focus on Vocabulary

Discount Stores

What are the names of the popular discount stores in your area? Which ones have you been to? What kinds of things could you find in each of the departments listed below?

DIRECTORY

AREA
- 1 Automotive
- 2 Hardware
- 4 Cleaning Supplies
- 4 Housewares
- 5 Appliances
- 9 Health and Beauty
- 15 Jewelry
- 20-21 Furniture
- 17 Accessories
- 13 Toys and Games
- 3 Bath and Bedding
- 6-8 Men's and Boys' Clothing
- 10-12 Women's and Girls' Clothing
- 14 Sporting Goods
- 16 Shoes and Hosiery
- 18 Electronics
- 19 Pharmacy
- 22 Music and Videos

8 In which departments of a discount store can you find each of the items listed below? Look at the Focus on Vocabulary box above. Write the name of the department for each item below. Then check your answers with a partner.

Items	Department
1. basketballs	
2. hairbrushes	
3. socks	
4. watches	
5. paper towels	
6. pillows	
7. screwdrivers	
8. car wax	
9. tennis shoes	
10. batteries	
11. coffee makers	

9 With a partner, ask and answer how to find the departments below. Ask, "Excuse me. Where's the hardware department?" Start at the checkouts.

Example: A: Where's the hardware department?
B: You go past the shoes and turn left. Go to the end of the store and you'll see the hardware department on the right.

1. Hardware
2. Furniture
3. Bath and Bedding
4. Electronics
5. Books

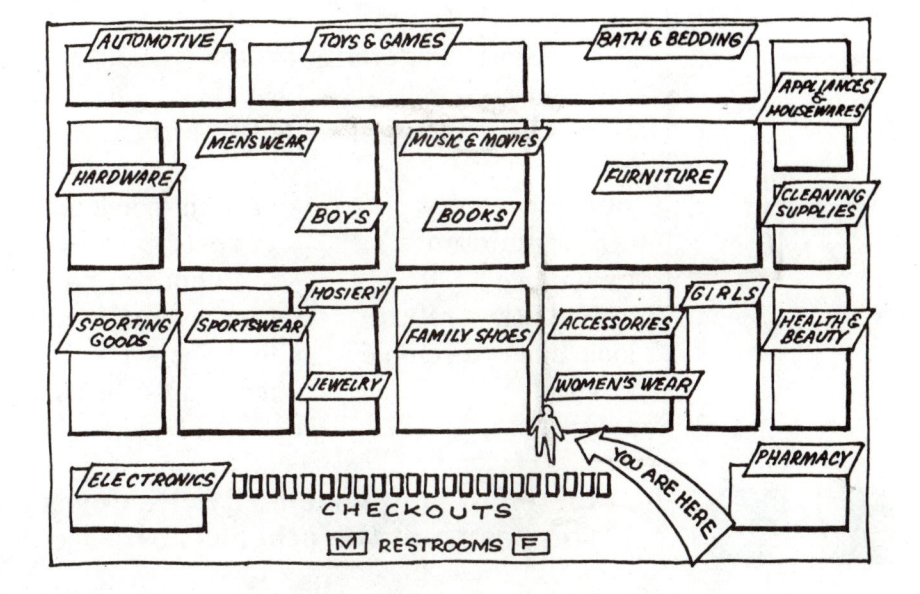

10 Work with a partner. Imagine that you need to buy each of the items below, but you don't know where to find them. Take turns role-playing the customer and the salesperson.

You need to buy:
1. a new oil filter for your car
2. a wallet for your mother
3. a calculator
4. a bilingual dictionary
5. a pair of sweat pants
6. a board game
7. a baseball bat
8. a prescription medicine
9. a CD
10. a coffee maker

Example: Customer: Can you tell me where I can find _____?
Salesperson: That's in the _____ department.

Unit 10   103

Inseparable Two-Word Verbs

Many two-word verbs are separable. You can separate the two parts.

Helena is **picking up** her son. Helena is **picking** her son **up**.

Some two-word verbs are inseparable. You cannot separate the two parts.

Gloria is **getting on** the bus. NOT *Gloria is getting the bus on.

Here are some inseparable two-word verbs:

run into = meet
(an acquaintance)
by chance
come back = return
look like = resemble

call on = ask someone to speak in class
get over = recover, get better from an illness, a shock, a bad experience
turn around = turn one's body
look for = try to find
grow up = become an adult

11 Listen to your teacher. Write down only the two-word verbs that you hear, not the other verbs.

1. _____   4. _____
2. _____   5. _____
3. _____   6. _____

12 Gloria wrote a letter in English to her cousin Mercedes, who is an English teacher in Mexico City. She wanted to show Mercedes how well she knows English. Read Gloria's letter and circle the two-word verbs.

> Dear Mercedes,
> When I come back to Mexico City, you'll be surprised how good my English is. I'm taking English classes at school near my apartment. I go to class twice a week, and the teacher likes me. She calls on me all the time, and usually I know the answer. I like her, too. She looks like that actress in the movie we saw before I left. (I don't remember the title.)
> I ran into Enrique three days ago. I was in a store downtown, and I turned around and saw him. He said hello. He looked happy, but I don't think he has completely gotten over that terrible illness he had. He still looks a bit sick.
> Well, now I just have to look for a stamp and mail this. Give my love to everyone. Write soon.
>
> Love,
> Gloria

13 Look at the pictures below. On a separate sheet of paper, write a sentence with an inseparable two-word verb for each picture. Use the verbs listed below. One of the verbs is not needed.
needed.

run into   look for   come back   call on   look like

14 Now work with a partner. Compare your sentences from Exercise 13. Correct any errors you find. Then share your sentences with the class.

15 Complete these sentences with two-word verbs from the grammar box on page 104.

1. People always say Keiko _____ her mother. They have the same eyes and smile.

2. Tan was very surprised to see Yoshiko at the zoo. He didn't expect to _____ anyone he knew there.

3. Tan had a bad cold last week. He is just starting to feel better. It took a long time to _____ that cold.

4. Yoshiko is often embarrassed when Jean _____ her in class.

Unit 10   105

Use What You Know

Think about places in or near your school, such as drinking fountains, restrooms, or the library. Write directions below from your classroom to a place in or near the school. Read your directions aloud. Your classmates will guess the destination you are thinking of.

_____
_____
_____
_____
_____
_____
_____

Wrapping Up

Find someone for each of the things listed below. Ask questions with *do* or *did*. When someone answers yes to a question, write his or her name on the correct line. Try to find a different name for each thing.

Example: A: Do you look like your mother?
B: Yes, I do. OR No, I don't.
A: Did you recently get over a cold?
B: Yes, I did. OR No, I didn't.

Name	Question
_____	looks like his/her mother
_____	recently got over a cold
_____	came back to school after being out of school for years
_____	usually takes off right after class
_____	looked for a new place to live this year
_____	looked up a word in the dictionary recently
_____	gets along with his/her neighbors very well
_____	ran into an old friend recently

♦ Modals of Probability
♦ Reflexive Pronouns
♦ Other Uses of Reflexive Pronouns
♦ Superlatives

Unit 11   Who's the oldest person alive?

Jean and her students are having a barbecue. What do you think they are talking about?

Setting the Scene

Gloria: Here's an interesting story about the oldest person in the world. How old do you think he is?
Helena: Oh, the oldest person might be about 100 years old.
Amir: No, he must be older than that—110 or 115 at least.
Gloria: You're both wrong. The oldest person is 120!
Helena: Wow! That's really hard to believe!

Modals of Probability

A: The phone is ringing.
B: That **must** be Victor. Almost certainly 95%
   should   Probably
   may   Quite possibly
   could/might   Possibly   30%

If you are almost 100% sure who is at the door, you can say, "That *will* be Victor." If you are not sure who is there but you think that maybe it's Victor, you can say, "That *might* be Victor" or "That *could* be Victor."

It **will** be cold tomorrow. Certainly   100%
   should   Probably
   may   Quite possibly
   could/might   Possibly   30%

When you say, "It *will* be cold," you are 100% sure it's going to be cold. When you're not so sure, you can say, "It *might* be cold" or "It *could* be cold."

1 Listen to the sentences. Put a check under *Certainly*, *Probably*, *Quite Possibly*, or *Possibly* for the information you hear in each sentence.

	Certainly	Probably	Quite Possibly	Possibly
1.	_____	_____	_____	_____
2.	_____	_____	_____	_____
3.	_____	_____	_____	_____
4.	_____	_____	_____	_____

2 Work with a partner. Rewrite each sentence below using a modal of probability from the grammar box on page 108. There are many possible answers.

Example: *There is a 10% chance of snow in Chicago tomorrow.*
It might snow tomorrow in Chicago.

1. There is an 80% chance of rain in Seattle later today.

   _____

2. There is a 30% chance of snow in Minneapolis tonight.

   _____

3. There is a 15% chance of a hurricane off the coast of Florida this weekend.

   _____

4. There is a 90% chance of clear, sunny skies in Tucson today.

   _____

5. There is a 50% chance of a tornado in the Midwest later in the week.

   _____

3 Listen to these predictions. Write each prediction below. Then write a percent to tell how sure each prediction is.

Example: *There will be an increase in property taxes next year.*
100% sure.

1. _____
2. _____
3. _____
4. _____

4 What are your predictions for the future? Write them on the lines below. Use modals of probability. Then share your predictions with a group.

Example: *Will there be a woman president of the U.S.?*
We think there will not be a woman president of the U.S. in the next 20 years.

1. Will there be an African-American president in the next election?
   _____

2. Will you (or your children) graduate from a U.S. college?
   _____

3. Will California have a major earthquake in the next ten years?
   _____

4. Will you buy a home computer in the next five years?
   _____

5 Work with a partner. Read each situation. Write a logical conclusion about each one. Compare answers with another pair of students. There are many possible correct answers.

Example: *My sister is usually very sweet and kind. Today she was angry and yelled at me for no reason.*
She must be in a bad mood today. She could be tired. She might be really busy with something.

1. Jean was not in class tonight.
   _____

2. Tan had three job interviews yesterday.
   _____

3. The baby's crying.
   _____

4. Gloria isn't eating anything at the barbecue.
   _____

5. Victor isn't paying attention in class.
   _____

Reflexive Pronouns

Sergio hurt **himself** when he was working on the deck.

I hurt **myself**.
You hurt **yourself**.
He hurt **himself**.
She hurt **herself**.
You hurt **yourselves**.
We hurt **ourselves**.
They hurt **themselves**.

You can use reflexive pronouns when the subject and the object are the same.

6 Read each sentence. Write the correct reflexive pronoun for each sentence.

Example: *Sergio had an accident last week. He hurt himself when he was fixing his car.*

1. Tan is studying ESL at night school. He knows he will learn to understand and speak English well. He believes in _____.

2. I cut _____ while I was shaving this morning.

3. Jean is teaching _____ to play the guitar.

4. Sometimes people talk to _____ when they are upset about something.

5. Yesterday Yoshiko's son, Yukio, hurt _____ in the kitchen. Yoshiko blamed _____ for the accident because she wasn't watching him at that moment.

6. We must teach _____ to have patience with young children.

Unit 11   111

Other Uses of Reflexive Pronouns

There are some other uses of reflexive pronouns.
Here are some special expressions:

Jean helped **herself** to a soda.
(*help yourself to something = serve yourself something*)

Sergio and his family enjoyed **themselves** at the barbecue.
(*enjoy yourself = have a good time*)

Helena lives **by herself**. (*alone*)
Jean likes to go to movies **by herself**. (*alone*)
By + reflexive pronoun = *alone*

7 Write the missing words in each sentence below. Use the expressions below with the correct reflexive pronoun.

help yourself   enjoy yourself   by yourself

Example: *Jean and Gloria went to a movie last weekend. They really enjoyed themselves.*

1. Helena is afraid to take the bus _____ after dark.

2. Jean and Ana had dinner at a salad bar. They _____ to different kinds of salads.

3. Jean _____ at her birthday party last month.

4. Tan's daughter, Thuy, often plays _____.

5. Amir _____ to a piece of chicken at the barbecue.

8 Read the six questions below. Think about your answers to the questions. Make a few notes to help you tell your answers to a partner. Then share your answers with a partner.

1. When did you help yourself to something?
2. When did you enjoy yourself recently?
3. What do you like to do when you are by yourself?
4. What did you like to do by yourself when you were young?
5. What is easy for you to do by yourself?
6. What is difficult for you to do by yourself?

9. Work in a group. Take turns telling each other your answers to the questions in Exercise 8. In your group, decide which of your answers are the most interesting and then share these answers with the class.

Superlatives

You can use superlative adjectives or adverbs to compare three or more people or things.

Superlatives with *the . . . -est*:
Tan is **the oldest** student in the class.
Ana works **the longest** hours.
Gloria is **the funniest** person in the class.

Use *the . . . -est* with
1. one-syllable adjectives or adverbs: *the oldest, the longest*
2. adjectives that end in *y*: *the funniest*

Superlatives with *the most*:
Yoshiko writes **the most carefully** of all Jean's students.
Amir has **the most beautiful** gold chain you've ever seen.
Is English **the most useful** language?

Use *the most* with
1. adjectives with two or more syllables: *beautiful, useful*
2. *-ly* adverbs: *carefully*

Irregular Superlatives

	Comparative	**Superlative**
good, well	better	the best
bad, badly	worse	the worst
little	less	the least
much, many	more	the most
far	farther	the farthest

See Appendix page 174 for spelling rules.

10 Gloria and the other students learned many new things from the *Guinness Book of World Records.* Fill in the missing superlatives from the facts they learned. Use the following adjectives: *high, bad, fast, poisonous, heavy, expensive, long, many.*

Example: *The _____ woman on earth is Florence Griffith Joyner, from the U.S. She can run 10 meters in 10 minutes and 49 seconds.*

1. The _____ airplane in the world is the supersonic *Concorde*, from France. It flies 1,450 miles per hour.

2. The _____ nonstop flight is from Los Angeles, California, to Sydney, Australia. The flight lasts almost 15 hours!

3. The _____ man in the world is Albert Jackson, from Mississippi. He weighs 891 pounds. He has a 120-inch chest, a 116-inch waist, and 70-inch thighs.

4. The _____ diamond ever sold was a 101-carat, pear-shaped diamond. It was sold in Switzerland for $12,760,000 in 1990.

5. The _____ animal in the world is the golden poison-dart frog. An adult has enough poison to kill 1,500 people.

6. The _____ paid TV performer in 1991 was Bill Cosby. He earned about $115 million.

7. The country with the _____ people is China. It had about 1,151,300,000 people in 1991. About 44,000 Chinese babies are born every day.

8. The _____ disaster in the history of the world was the Black Death, or bubonic plague. About 75,000,000 people died from this disease from 1347 to 1351.

11 Work in groups. Decide which person in the group fits each description below. Complete the sentences with their names. Then share your most interesting sentences with the class.

1. _____ is the youngest.

2. _____ has lived in the U.S. the longest time.

3. _____ has the most children.

4. _____ has lived in the most different countries.

5. _____ has the most unusual job.

Small Talk: Giving and Receiving Compliments

In the United States, people often give compliments to be friendly. Sometimes people use superlatives when they give compliments. For example, someone might say, "You have the most beautiful skin," or "You are the best cook in the world." The appropriate response to a compliment is "Thank you." Here are some examples.

A: You have the prettiest smile.
B: Thank you.

A: That was the best meal I've eaten in months.
B: It's nice of you to say that.

A: I love your earrings. They're the most unusual earrings I've ever seen.
B: Why, thank you. They're from India.

A: You are the most intelligent woman I've ever met.
B: Thank you.

12 With a partner, practice giving and receiving compliments like the ones in Small Talk above.

Partnerwork ▶ Person A

Work with a partner. Person A looks at this page only. Person B looks at page 116 only.

Look at the two pictures below. The pictures show Victor at home. Your partner's pictures are a little different from your pictures. Ask questions like the ones below to find the differences between your pictures and your partner's pictures. Write down the differences you find.

Example: *What will Victor do today? Why?*
What should Victor do today? Why?
What might Victor do today? Why?

Unit 11   115

Partnerwork ▶ Person B

Work with a partner. Person B looks at this page only. Person A looks at page 115 only.

Look at the two pictures below. The pictures show Victor at home. Your partner's pictures are a little different from your pictures. Ask questions like the ones below to find the differences between your pictures and your partner's pictures. Write down the differences you find.

Example: *What will Victor do today? Why?*
What should Victor do today? Why?
What might Victor do today? Why?

In Your Own Words

Write a short paragraph about yourself. Choose one of the following topics:
- The time I enjoyed myself the most in the U.S.
- The time I hurt myself really badly.

Then share your writing with a group.

Wrapping Up

Write predictions about the future of your classmates and teacher. Then share your predictions with the class.

Example: *I think Tan will be the richest person in our class because he works very hard and he never gives up.*

1. I think _____ might have the most grandchildren because _____.

2. I think _____ could become the most famous person in our class because _____.

3. I think _____ will _____

_____.

116   Unit 11

- Present Perfect Simple and Continuous
- Review of Comparatives and Superlatives
- Comparisons with *As* + Adjective + *As*

Unit 12   Which one is more expensive?

What is Amir doing? Have you ever done this?

Setting the Scene

Amir: I've been looking for a car, Sergio. But they're more expensive than I can afford.

Sergio: Have you looked in *Auto Mart*? The cheapest cars are in that paper.

Amir: I've been looking through *Auto Mart* all day. But used cars are almost as expensive as new ones! I've always wanted a new car, but I'm not sure I can afford one. What would you do, Sergio?

Sergio: I'd buy a used car.

Present Perfect Simple and Continuous

I've read that book. ≠ **I've been reading** that book.
(finished)   (unfinished)

You can use the present perfect continuous for actions begun in the past and unfinished in the present.

I've had breakfast (already). ≠ **I've been having** breakfast (every day at seven).

(finished)   (unfinished, repeated)

You can also use the present perfect continuous for repeated actions begun in the past and continued in the present.

How long **have** you **been living** here? = How long **have** you **lived** here?
I've been working here for five years. = **I've worked** here for five years.

You can use the present perfect simple for actions that are finished at the present moment. You can use the present perfect simple or the present perfect continuous for actions that started in the past and continue in the present or for actions repeated up to the present.

> Don't use stative verbs in the present perfect continuous.

Unit 12

1. Think of two things you've finished doing in class today and two things you've been doing in class today. Write about these things below.

   Example: Finished   Unfinished

   1. read the conversation   study the present perfect
   2. _____   _____
   3. _____   _____

2. Now tell a partner what you have done and what you have been doing. Use your answers from Exercise 1. Use the present perfect simple for finished actions and the present perfect continuous for unfinished actions.

   Example: *I've read the dialogue at the beginning of the unit.*
   I've been studying the present perfect.

3. Imagine it is 5:00 P.M. What have the people in the pictures below been doing all day? On a separate sheet of paper, write what they have done (finished actions) and what they have been doing (unfinished or repeated actions) today.

4. Work with a partner. Take turns asking questions about the people's jobs in Exercise 3. Ask as many questions as you can.

   Example: A: What has the woman been doing all day?
             B: She's been driving a bus.
             A: How many passengers has she picked up?
             B: About a hundred.

5 What are some things you have been doing repeatedly since you came to the United States? Write these things on a separate piece of paper.

   Example: *I've been taking ESL classes every week. I've been doing a lot of homework.*

   Now share your sentences with a partner. Take turns asking how many times you have done those things. Then tell the class one thing about your partner.

   Example: *How many classes have you had? How many homework assignments have you done this week?*

6 With a partner, talk about how your life has changed since you came to the U.S. For example, talk about the things you have been doing, the things you have done successfully, or how long you have been living where you are living. Write down what your partner tells you and tell the class about him or her.

Review of Comparatives and Superlatives

You have learned many ways to compare people and things:

-er	I am tall**er** than my mother.
more	My mother is **more understanding** than I am.
-est	I am the fast**est** runner in my family.
most	My grandmother is the **most intelligent** person I've ever met.

7 Work with a partner. Take turns asking and answering questions with the words below. Use *-er, more, -est, most,* or irregular comparatives or superlatives in your questions and answers.

   Example: *good athlete   family*
   - A: Are you the best athlete in your family?
   - B: No, my dad is the best athlete in our family.

   1. good athlete—   your family
   2. good cook—   your family
   3. tall person—   your class
   4. young—   your town
   5. energetic—   your school

Connections: Talking About Change

The Pessimist:
Things are more expensive than they used to be. Prices have been going up, but quality has been going down. Unemployment has been rising. Salaries have been dropping. The cost of living has been rising, and taxes are higher. Everything has gotten much worse.

The Optimist:
Technology is better than it used to be. We've made fantastic progress in medicine. We've controlled terrible diseases such as polio and tuberculosis. Transportation and communication have been getting better too. Life has gotten much easier.

You can use comparatives and the present perfect simple and continuous to talk about change.

8 With a partner, role-play a conversation like the one above. One of you can be the optimist, and the other can be the pessimist. Think of as many ideas as possible. Write them down and share them with a group.

9 With a partner, think of things that are better and worse in your native countries than ten years ago. Write your ideas below. Then share your ideas with the class. See if your classmates agree with your ideas.

		Country 1	Country 2
Better	1	_____	_____
	2	_____	_____
	3	_____	_____
Worse	1	_____	_____
	2	_____	_____
	3	_____	_____

Unit 12

Comparisons with As + Adjective + As

You can use *as . . . as* to compare things that are exactly the same in some way.

A small new car is **as expensive as** a used luxury car.

You can use *almost as . . . as* or *nearly as . . . as* to compare two things that are almost the same.

Keiko is **almost as tall as** her mother.

You can use *not as . . . as* to compare things that are similar but not exactly the same.

Tan thinks English is **not as difficult as** Chinese.

10   Below is a photograph of Sergio and his cousin Alonso. Sergio is on the right. Read the sentences below and write the missing words in the lines. Use *as . . . as*, *almost as . . . as*, and *not as . . . as*. Compare answers with a partner.

Alonso—age: 26; height: 5 feet 6 inches; weight: 140 pounds

Sergio—age: 25; height: 5 feet 6 inches; weight: 135 pounds

Example: *Sergio is as not as old as as Alonso.*

1. Sergio is _____ old _____ his cousin.

2. Sergio is _____ heavy _____ Alonso.

3. Alonso's nose is _____ big _____ Sergio's.

4. Sergio is _____ tall _____ Alonso.

122   Unit 12

11 Work with a partner. Look through magazines for pictures of two people. The people must be similar but not exactly the same. Write a story about the people. Use the following expressions: *as . . . as*, *almost as . . . as*, and *not as . . . as*. Tell your story to a small group. Then choose one or two stories from each group to tell the class.

12 Work in groups. Each person makes up a sentence about someone in the class. Use *as . . . as*, *almost as . . . as*, or *not as . . . as* in your sentence. When it is your turn, repeat all the other students' sentences before adding yours.

Example: Yoshiko: Chan Ho is almost as old as Tan.
Amir: Chan Ho is almost as old as Tan. Jean's hair isn't as long as Gloria's.
Victor: Chan Ho is almost as old as Tan. Jean's hair isn't as long as Gloria's. Sergio's spelling is almost as bad as mine.

13 Read the sentences below. Use comparative adjectives to write a new sentence with the same meaning. Then compare your sentences with a partner.

Example: *Teenagers aren't as careful as adults.* Adults are more careful than teenagers.

1. Crackers aren't as fattening as cookies.

   _____

2. New Orleans isn't as cold as Chicago in the winter.

   _____

3. New York isn't as big as Tokyo.

   _____

4. The population of India isn't as big as the population of China.

   _____

Unit 12

Focus on Vocabulary

Descriptive Comparisons

To describe people or things, you can use expressions with animal or object names. Write the correct words on the lines.

1. This baby never cries. She's as quiet as a _____.

2. Jean doesn't need help to lift this big box. It's as light as a _____.

3. Tan played soccer all afternoon. Now he's as hungry as a _____.

4. This bed is very uncomfortable. It's as hard as a _____.

5. Gloria likes to do things her way. She doesn't listen to advice from other people. She's as stubborn as a _____.

6. Helena doesn't have to work today. She feels as free as a _____.

bird   rock   mouse

feather   bear   mule

14 What expressions from your native language are like the ones above? Make a list and tell the class.

Example: *In Ecuador, we say "free as a butterfly."*

_____
_____
_____

Small Talk: It's as simple as that

Sometimes *as . . . as* is not a real comparison. For example, "It's as simple as that" means "There's nothing more to say."

We need a strong defense, Tanya. It's as simple as that.

As simple as what?

15 Read the sentences below. Do you agree or disagree with each sentence? Write agree or disagree next to each sentence. If you disagree with a sentence, rewrite it on a separate piece of paper. Change the sentence so that you agree with it. Then work with a group. Compare your opinions and discuss them.

1. Foreign cars are better than American cars.
2. Intelligence is not as important as beauty.
3. American children are more disrespectful than Asian children.
4. Women are not as strong as men.
5. The most beautiful beaches in the world are on the Mediterranean Sea.
6. Air pollution is not as bad in the U.S. as in Europe.
7. It is easier to understand English than to speak it.
8. Public schools are as good as private schools.
9. English is not as difficult to learn as Arabic.

Use What You Know

Choose one of the topics below and answer the questions on a separate piece of paper. Then form a group with classmates who wrote about the same topic. Discuss your answers with your group.

Topics:

Customs: How are American customs and traditions different from the customs and traditions in your native country? How are they similar?

Food and clothes: How are American food and clothes different from the food and clothes in your native country? How are they similar?

Family: How are American families different from families in your native country? How are they similar? In what ways do you take after your parents? How are you different from them?

Schools and teachers: How are American schools and teachers different from schools and teachers in your native country? How are they similar?

Wrapping Up

Find someone who has done each of the things below. When someone answers yes to a question, write his or her name next to that thing. Try to find a different name for each question. Write the names on your paper. If you don't know how to spell your classmates' names, ask them.

Example: A: Have you been bored in class this week?
B: Yes, I have. OR No, I haven't.

_____ has been having a good week

_____ has been having a bad week

_____ has been studying English as long as you have

_____ has not been studying English as long as you have

_____ has been working at his or her job a long time

_____ has not been working at his or her job a long time

Review: Units 10–12

1. As a class, brainstorm all the two-word verbs you can. Then identify which verbs are separable and which verbs are inseparable. Divide the class into two teams. Take turns making up sentences using verbs from the board. As you use the verbs, cross them out on the board.

2. Work with a partner. Write a conversation using as many two-word verbs as possible. Use separable and inseparable verbs. After each pair presents its conversation to the class, write down the two-word verbs you hear.

3. Think about what you did yesterday. Use two-word verbs to tell about what you did. Write three sentences. Then share your sentences with a group.

4. Work in a group. Discuss the situations below. Think of a logical reason for each situation. Use modals of probability.

    Example: *Tan has been having trouble sleeping.*
    He must be worried about finding a new job.

    1. Helena has been working overtime every day this week.

    2. Victor has been speaking English every day.

5. On a card, write two things you like to do by yourself. Put all the cards into a bag. Take a new card from the bag and find the person who likes to do both of the things on the card. When you find the person, write his or her name on the card. Then tell the class about your classmate.

    Example: Card: I like to take walks by myself.
    A: Do you like to take walks by yourself?
    B: Yes, I do. OR No, I don't.

6 Work with a partner. Compare yourself with your partner in as many ways as you can think of. Share your information with another pair of students.

Example: *Who is taller?*
Who is older?
Who is heavier?
Who is from a smaller family?
Who has been studying English longer?
Who arrived in the U.S. more recently?
Who is more patient?
Who is more comfortable with American culture and customs?

7 Work in a group. Discuss the questions below. Compare all your classmates. Then match each of the questions below with a student in your class. Share your choices with the class.

1. Who is the most dedicated student?
2. Who is the friendliest student?
3. Who is the funniest student?
4. Who is the shiest student?
5. Who is the youngest student?
6. Who is the newest student?
7. Who has been studying English the longest?
8. Who has the most children?

- Past Continuous
- Past Continuous: Questions and Negative Statements
- Simple Past/Past Continuous with *When* and *While*

Unit 13   I was walking down Park Street when it happened

What has just happened? Has this ever happened to you?

Setting the Scene

Officer: What happened?
Amir: Well, I was just walking down Park Street when I heard a crash. The car hit the streetlight, and the driver jumped out and ran.
Officer: Did you see his face?
Amir: Not really. But while I was waiting for the police, I heard someone say the driver was a man in his twenties with red hair.

Past Continuous

Eight years ago, Helena **was living** in Poland.
Yesterday at two o'clock, Tan **was waiting** to talk to a social worker.

I / He / She	**was living** in Mexico.	We / You / They	**were living** in Mexico.

You can use the past continuous (past of *be* + *-ing*) to talk about an action that was in progress in the past.

1 Listen to the sentences. Write the past continuous verbs that you hear in each sentence.

1. _____   4. _____
2. _____   5. _____
3. _____   6. _____

2 What were you doing _____ years ago? Finish the sentences below. Then share your sentences with a partner.

Example: *One year ago today, I was working for my father in Peru.*

1. One year ago today, _____.
2. Three years ago today, _____.
3. Five years ago today, _____.
4. Ten years ago today, _____.

3   Work in groups. Look at a newspaper. Each person finds a story or a picture about a person in the news. Take turns asking questions about what the person was doing.

Example: A: Here's a really interesting story about the vice president of the U.S.
B: What was he doing yesterday?
A: He was visiting Japan.

Past Continuous: Questions and Negative Statements

| What **were** | you
we
they | **doing**? | What **was** | I
he
she | **doing**? |

| I
He
She | **wasn't reading**. | We
You
They | **weren't reading**. |

A: **What were you doing** yesterday at two o'clock?
B: I was watching a game on TV.

A: I saw you this morning. You were reading the *Daily News* at the bus stop.
B: **I wasn't reading** the *Daily News*. I was reading the *Times*.

A: I heard what you said to Rachel.
B: Really? **Were you listening** to our conversation?

4   Work with a partner. Choose a day of the week and a time. Ask your partner what he or she was doing at that time on that day. If your partner can't remember, you can ask if he or she was doing one of the following activities.

study	play basketball	play cards	clean the apartment
shop	do laundry	work	lift weights
read	do the dishes	watch TV	ride the bus/subway

Example: Kamil: Jorge, what were you doing on Tuesday at five o'clock?
Jorge: I don't remember.
Kamil: Were you playing cards?
Jorge: No, I wasn't. I think I was cooking dinner.

Focus on Vocabulary

Phrases for Describing People

A: Who's that woman with glasses?
B: Do you mean the woman with the briefcase?
A: No, I mean the woman with the dark curly hair.
B: Oh, that's Rosa. She's a new student.

You can describe people by talking about what they are **wearing** (clothing, jewelry, glasses, etc.), what they are **carrying or holding** (bags, briefcases, etc.), or what kind of **physical characteristics** they have (hair color, hair length, eye color, etc.).

a striped shirt   a plaid skirt

Here are some phrases for describing people:

in the	striped	shirt	with	brown hair	with the	briefcase
	plaid	suit		blond		purse
	blue	jacket		black		cane
	gray	skirt		red		shopping bag
		dress		gray		umbrella
		blouse		curly		book bag
		pants		straight		hat

A: Do you see that man in the striped shirt?
B: The one with brown hair?
A: Yes. That's my brother.

You can use phrases with preposition + adjective + noun to describe people that you see.

5 Work with a partner. Use phrases in the Focus on Vocabulary box to describe some of the students in your class, but don't tell your partner who you are talking about. Let your partner guess from the description you give.

Example: *I'm thinking of a woman in our class. She's the one with glasses and brown hair, in the white blouse.*

6 Each student in the class will find and cut out a picture of an interesting person from a magazine or newspaper. Write a description of the person in your picture. Use the expressions from page 132. Do not show your description to anyone. Then put all the pictures on a table in the classroom or tape all the pictures to the board. Take turns reading your descriptions aloud. Your classmates will guess which person you wrote about.

Example: *It's a woman with a blue shirt and black pants, with curly black hair and a shopping bag.*

Connections: More Ways to Describe People

What did the thief look like?

He was a man in his thirties. He had short red hair and sunglasses. He was wearing a denim jacket, a white T-shirt, and jeans.

To describe age, use phrases like *in his/her teens, twenties, thirties, forties, fifties,* etc. To talk about physical characteristics, use *have*: *Rosa has short curly hair.* To talk about clothing, use *wear* in the present continuous or past continuous: *He is/was wearing a denim jacket. She is/was wearing a white blouse.* To describe someone unknown to your listener, use *a/an*, not *the*, before the noun.

7 Describe some classmates to a partner. Add details like the ones in Connections above.

Example: *I'm thinking of a man in our class. He has gray hair and glasses. He's in his forties. He's wearing a striped shirt and sneakers.*

Your partner will guess who it is.

Simple Past/Past Continuous with *When*

Amir **was walking** down the street **when** the car **hit** the streetlight.
    (action in progress)   (interrupting action)
When the car **hit** the streetlight, Amir **was walking** down the street.
    (interrupting action)   (action in progress)

When can connect two actions. Use the past continuous to talk about an action in progress in the past. Use the simple past to talk about an action that interrupts the first action.

8 Work with a partner. Talk about what was happening (in progress) when something else happened (interrupted the first action or situation) in the pictures below. Then write a sentence about each two pictures.

Chou

1. clean the bathroom   2. fall

Alla

1. serve lunch   2. spill the soup

134   Unit 13

9   What happened in the pictures below? Complete the sentences. Use verbs in the simple past and the continuous. Then compare your answers with a group. Do you agree or disagree? There are many possible answers.

1. Jean _____ when the car _____ a flat tire.

2. The hotel employees _____ and _____ clothes when Gloria _____.

3. Jean _____ a cup of coffee when Ana _____.

Unit 13   135

Simple Past/Past Continuous with *While*

Jean's brother **painted** her house **while** Jean **was traveling** in South America.
                (shorter action)   (longer action)

While means *during the time that*. When talking about past actions or situations, you can use *while* to connect a shorter action (in the simple past) to a longer action (in the past continuous).

You can also put the *while* clause first:

While Jean **was traveling**, her brother **painted** her house.
      (longer action)   (shorter action)

10 Finish each sentence. Add a shorter action. Use the simple past. Share your best two sentences with a partner.

Example: *While I was growing up, my country went through a civil war.*

1. While I was growing up, _____.

2. While I was preparing to come to this country, _____
   _____.

3. While the teacher was explaining the lesson, _____
   _____.

4. While I was waiting for the bus, _____.

5. While I was standing in line at the grocery store, _____
   _____.

6. While my children were growing up, _____.

11 Think about yesterday. What happened while you were doing something else? Draw pictures in the boxes below to show what you were doing. Tell a partner.

12 Now exchange textbooks with a different partner. Look at your partner's pictures from Exercise 11 and write sentences about them. Use the past continuous and the simple past. Your partner will do the same with your pictures. Share your sentences with another pair.

13 Choose the correct form, past continuous or simple past.

1. While Pierre (*wait*) _____ in line, someone (*start*) _____ to hum a song he knew.

2. While Patricia (*stand*) _____ at the bus stop, a singer nearby (*sing*) _____ an entire aria from *Carmen*.

3. An artist (*draw*) _____ two portraits while Jessica (*eat*) _____ lunch at a sidewalk cafe.

Partnerwork ▶ Person A

Work with a classmate. Person A looks at this picture only. Person B looks at the picture on page 138 only.

The picture shows Jean and her students at a party, but some of the faces are missing. Find out the names of the people you don't know by asking your partner questions.

Example: A: Who dropped a cup of coffee while Sergio was drawing?
B: Do you mean the woman in the light dress?
A: Yes.
B: That's Jean.

Partnerwork ▶ Person B

Work with a classmate. Person B looks at this picture only. Person A looks at the picture on page 137 only.

The picture shows Jean and her students at a party, but some of the faces are missing. Find out the names of the people you don't know by asking your partner questions.

Example: B: Who was dancing with Chan Ho?
A: Do you mean the woman in the dark dress?
B: Yes.
A: That's Helena.

In Your Own Words

Think about your journey to the U.S. Write about it on a separate sheet of paper. Then share it with a group or the class.

Wrapping Up

In a group, write a story about the pictures. Make up an ending to the story and tell the class.

- Relative Clauses with *Who*, *Which*, and *That*
- Relative Clauses: Word Order

Unit 14 What a surprise!

Where are Tan and Chan Ho? What are they doing there?

Setting the Scene

Chan Ho: Tan! What a surprise!
Tan: Chan Ho! Hi! I just had a job interview.
Chan Ho: What kind of job is it?
Tan: A caseworker. The city needs people who are bilingual. It's a job that interests me. Also, I need a job which has good benefits.
Chan Ho: A job that has good benefits is hard to find.

Relative Clauses with *Who*

Chan Ho saw a friend **who** was applying for job.

They need to hire people **who** are bilingual.

If the word before *who* is singular, use a singular verb after *who*. If the word before *who* is plural, use a plural verb after *who*.

1. What do you know about the people in Jean's ESL class? Complete the sentences below. There are many possible answers for each sentence.

   Example: *Jean has a student who used to be an opera singer. Her name is Helena.*

   1. Jean has a student who _____.

      Her name is Yoshiko.

   2. Jean has a friend who _____.

      Her name is Ana Rivera.

   3. Jean has two students who _____.

      Their names are Victor and Gloria.

   4. Jean has a student who _____.

      His name is Sergio.

   5. Jean has two students who _____.

      Their names are Tan and Chan Ho.

2 Now work with a group and compare your answers from Exercise 1. See if your answers are the same or different. Correct any errors you find.

3 Work with a group. Tell the group about some of your friends or relatives who do interesting things or have interesting hobbies. Then tell the class.

Example: *I have a cousin who plays the violin in an orchestra. I have some friends who collect stamps from all over the world.*

4 Look at the pictures below. With a partner, make sentences matching people with activities. You can use the following model. Many different sentences are possible.

Example: *Jack is a neighbor who plays the guitar.*

Jack—neighbor    Janet—friend    Hal—cousin    Lucia—co-worker

plays the guitar 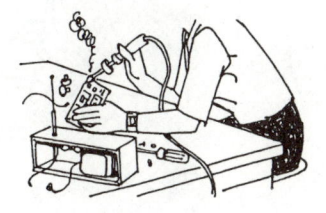   makes radios    plays golf a lot    likes to go scuba diving

Then tell your partner about a neighbor, friend, cousin, or co-worker you have.

Unit 14   141

Focus on Vocabulary

Jobs

Here are some jobs in the U.S. Look at the pictures below. Do you know anyone who has these jobs?

Day-care worker

Bodyguard

Reporter

Gardener

Construction worker

Illustrator

Dental hygienist

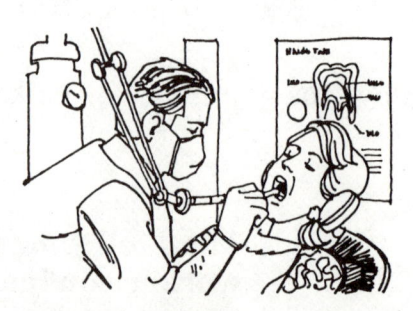

Dentist

5 Look at the vocabulary on page 142. Match the jobs with the job descriptions below. Complete the job descriptions with the word *who* and the correct verb from the following list. Note that three of these verbs and three job titles are not used.

| protect | interview | clean | draw |
| water | build | fill | watch |

1. The successful _____ loves children. This is a person _____ _____ and cares for children at work every day.

2. A good _____ knows everything about teeth. He or she knows the name of every tooth in a person's mouth. This professional is a person _____ _____ cavities and does more difficult work when necessary.

3. A successful _____ loves news and current events. He or she needs to know everything about what is happening in the world or in his or her community. This is a person _____ _____ people to get information.

4. A good _____ has a certain artistic talent. Some people work in black and white, and others work in color, or both. This is a person _____ _____ people and figures well.

5. An experienced _____ does a lot of heavy work. He or she often has to work in high places. This job can be dangerous. This person is a worker _____ _____ houses, offices, highways, and other things.

6 In a group, brainstorm a list of five jobs that you know about. Then write a description for each job. Use relative clauses with *who*.

7 Use your job descriptions from Exercise 6. Work with a different partner. In turns, role-play a job interview and tell your classmate what kind of person you need for the job that you are offering. Ask if your classmate has ever done this kind of work.

Example: A: We're looking for a gardener. We need someone who loves plants and who knows how to take care of them. Have you ever worked as a gardener?
B: No, I haven't worked as a gardener, but I would like to learn.

Unit 14

Relative Clauses with *Which* and *That*

Tan wants a job **which** has medical and dental benefits.
Tan wants a job **that** has medical and dental benefits.

You can use relative clauses with *which* and *that* to describe things.

Jean has a friend **that** works at the employment office.

You can also use *that* to describe people.

8 Work with a partner. Take turns talking about the things listed below. Talk about the things that you like. Use *that* or *which*. Agree or disagree with your partner's opinions.

Example: A: I like vacations *that last a long time*.
B: So do I. (*agreement*)
I don't. (*disagreement*)

B: I like food *that is hot and spicy*.
A: So do I. (*agreement*)
I don't. (*disagreement*)

1. vacations
2. food
3. houses
4. weekends
5. cities
6. hair
7. clothes
8. restaurants
9. cars

9 With a different partner, talk about things that you don't like. Use the list in Exercise 8. Use *that* or *which*. Agree or disagree with your partner's opinions.

Example: A: I don't like restaurants that are noisy.
B: I don't either. OR Neither do I. (*agreement*)
I do. (*disagreement*)

10 Listen to the sentences. Circle the words you hear. Underline any other words that are correct.

Example: *I'm happy to have a job that has medical insurance.*

    (that)   who   <u>which</u>

1. that   who   which
2. that   who   which
3. that   who   which
4. that   who   which
5. that   who   which

Relative Clauses: Word Order

Tan is a person **who likes English**.

The people **who got those jobs** were very lucky.

Some of the questions **that were on the forms** seemed strange to Tan.

Relative clauses can come at the end of a sentence or in the middle of a sentence.

11 Imagine you are a substitute teacher. Write six questions using *who* or *that* to learn the students' names in the class.

Example: *Who is the woman **who** is sitting right in front of the teacher's desk?*
*Who is the tall, thin man **that** is wearing a black sweater?*

1. _____
2. _____
3. _____
4. _____
5. _____
6. _____

12 Work with a partner. In turns, ask and answer your questions from Exercise 11, page 145.

Example: *Who is the woman **who** is sitting right in front of the teacher's desk?*
That's Helena, the woman from Poland.

13 Bring to class a photograph of some of your relatives or an interesting picture from a newspaper or magazine. Then tell a small group about your picture. Use relative clauses when possible.

Example: *The woman who is sitting down is my grandmother.*
The children who are playing are my nieces.
The man who is on the left is the president of Mexico.

Connections: Exclamations with *What* and *How*

What a surprise!
How nice to run into you, Tan!
What strange questions!

To show emotion, you can use exclamations with **what** and **how**.

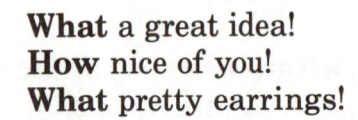

What a great idea!   **What** terrible news!
How nice of you!   **How** awful!
What pretty earrings!

14 Work with a partner. Read each of the situations below. Take turns making exclamations for the situations.

1. You see a beautiful sunset. You say, . . .

2. Your dog walks all over the house with muddy paws. You say, . . .

3. Your friend cooks you a delicious dinner. You say, . . .

4. Your neighbor shows you her new baby. You say, . . .

15 Listen to the sentences. Do you hear *a*, *an*, or no article in each exclamation? If you hear *a* or *an*, write the word on the lines below in the first column. If you don't hear an article, check the second column.

	a/an	no article
1.	_____	_____
2.	_____	_____
3.	_____	_____
4.	_____	_____
5.	_____	_____
6.	_____	_____
7.	_____	_____
8.	_____	_____
9.	_____	_____

Small Talk: Telling "White Lies"

A white lie is an untrue statement. People tell white lies when they don't want to hurt someone's feelings.

> How do you like my new hat?

> Oh, how nice.

> *What an awful hat.*

16 If possible, work in a group with people who are not from your native country. What are some things you'd tell "white lies" about? Brainstorm a list of situations when people tell "white lies" in your native country. Then share your answers with the class.

17 Work with the same group. Use your list from Exercise 16 to role-play several situations in which people tell "white lies." Perform your best conversation for the class.

Use What You Know

Work in a group. Read the unfinished sentences below. Take turns finishing the sentences with *who*, *that*, or *which*. Agree or disagree with your classmates' sentences. Then share your sentences with another group.

Example: A: I like people **who** are friendly and outgoing.
B: Me, too.
C: Not me. I like people **that** are quiet and shy.
D: Oh, I don't. I think people **who** are shy are boring.

1. I like teachers . . .
2. I get angry at people . . .
3. I like movies . . .
4. I like jobs . . .
5. I like friends . . .
6. I like weekends . . .
7. I don't like people . . .
8. I don't understand people . . .

Wrapping Up

Here are a few of the questions you might be asked in a job interview in the U.S. Match the questions with the answers below. Write the letter of the best answer on the correct line. Then compare your answers with a group of three to four students.

1. Why should we hire you for this position? _____
2. What are your strengths and weaknesses? _____
3. Why do you want to work for this company? _____
4. Is there anything else you'd like us to know about you? _____
5. Do you have any questions for us? _____

A. Well, I guess one of my best qualities is my persistence. I don't like to quit until the job is done—and done well. As for my greatest weakness, I guess sometimes I'm too shy.

B. Yes. I'd like you to know that I like to learn new things, and I learn quickly.

C. Yes. I'd like to know if there are any possibilities for advancement in the company.

D. As you can see from my resume and letters of recommendation, I have excellent training and a lot of experience in this area.

E. I know several people who work for this company. They like their jobs, and they like their co-workers. They also think the managers really care about the workers.

- Future with *Will* and *Won't*
- Future Conditional
- Factual Conditional
- Reflexive Pronouns/*Each other*

Unit 15   I'll miss you all!

Sergio, Jean, and Helena are talking about their plans for the summer. What do you think they will do?

Setting the Scene

Jean: What are your plans for the summer, Sergio? Are you doing anything special?
Sergio: Well, I've been accepted to the Art Institute school in Chicago. If I get a scholarship, I'll move there.
Helena: If the Art Institute accepts you, that means you have talent! Will you write to us from Chicago?
Sergio: Sure I'll write. I won't forget.
Jean: Let's all write to each other. I'll miss you all!

Future with *Will* and *Won't*

Promises: I'**ll be** careful. I **won't drive** fast.
Predictions: It **will** probably be very cold tomorrow.
Refusals: I **won't cut** my hair. I don't care what you say.
I **won't go** to that restaurant again. The food was awful.

You can use *will* and *won't* to talk about promises and predictions.
You can use *won't* to talk about things you refuse to do.

1 What do you think will happen to Jean and her students in the next few years? Write five predictions using *will* and *won't*.

Example: *Jean's friend Ana will become a famous writer.*

| Helena | Yoshiko | Sergio | Victor | Chan Ho |
| Amir | | Gloria | | Tan | | Jean |

1. _____
2. _____
3. _____
4. _____
5. _____

2 Work with a partner. Make predictions for your teacher and classmates. Write them below.

1. _____
2. _____
3. _____
4. _____
5. _____

3 In groups, share your predictions from Exercise 2. Choose three or four of the funniest or most interesting predictions from the group and share them with the class.

4 When we want to borrow something, we often promise to take good care of it and not lose it. Guess what promises Jean's students and their families are making in the situations below.

Example: *Tan's son wants to borrow his new jacket.*
   He says to Tan: I'll take it off when I eat, so I won't spill anything on it.

1. Sergio wants to borrow his father's car. What does he promise to do and not to do? He says:

   _____
   _____

2. Gloria would like to use her mother's camera. What does she promise to do and not to do? She says to her mother:

   _____
   _____

3. Keiko wants to use her dad's golf clubs. What does she promise to do and not to do? She says to her dad:

   _____
   _____

4. Yoshiko would like to borrow Victor's dictionary. What does she promise to do and not to do? She says to Victor:

   _____
   _____

Unit 15

Future Conditional

Present   *Future*

If you **don't hurry** up, we'**ll be** late.
  (first event)   (second event)

Future   *Present*

We'**ll be** late **if** you **don't hurry** up.
 (second event)   (first event)

You can use *will* in sentences with *if* when one thing can happen if something else happens first. The *if* clause describes the first possible event, which is the condition for the second possible event. The *will* clause describes the second possible event.

5 Complete the *will* clause of each sentence below. Make logical predictions. There are many possible answers. Then compare ideas with a classmate.

Example: *If Jean works too hard, she will probably get sick.*

1. If Sergio gets a scholarship to the Art Institute, he _____.
2. If Tan gets laid off again, he _____.
3. If Amir sells his house this month, he _____.
4. If Victor works in a dangerous neighborhood, he _____.
5. If Helena gets a part in the city opera, she _____.

6 Now complete the *if* clause of each sentence. Think of logical conditions. There are many possible answers. Then share your ideas with a classmate.

Example: *Yoshiko will be very angry if she doesn't improve her English.*

1. Victor will be very happy if he _____.
2. Helena will be very depressed if she _____.
3. Ana will quit her job if _____.
4. Chan Ho will go back to Korea if _____.
5. Yoshiko's husband will quit smoking if _____.
6. Jean will go to Mexico for summer vacation if _____.

7 Match the ideas in A and B to make logical sentences. Compare sentences with a partner.

Example: *If you eat dinner too late, you will have trouble sleeping.*
You will have trouble sleeping if you eat dinner too late.

A	B
1. eat dinner too late	save money
2. buy too many things on credit	feel exhausted
3. shop carefully	learn English faster
4. have two jobs and go to night school	always miss your native country
5. watch TV and listen to American music	have trouble sleeping
6. move to another country as an adult	have to pay high interest

Focus on Vocabulary

Weather Conditions

Here are some weather conditions. How many have you experienced?

a blizzard   a thunderstorm   a heat wave

a flood   a cold wave   a snowstorm

Here are some ways to talk about these conditions.
1. We're having a blizzard.
2. We're having a thunderstorm. We're having a storm. It's pouring.
3. We're having a heat wave.
4. We're having a flood. It's flooding.
5. We're having a cold wave. It's freezing. It's terribly cold.
6. We're having a snowstorm. It's snowing very hard.

When you talk about weather conditions in a future conditional sentence, the *if* clause takes the simple present: *If it snows, I'll stay home.*

8 Work with a partner. Read about the weather for different parts of the country in the newspaper. Choose three places and imagine you are there. Talk about the weather conditions in those places.

Factual Conditional

If you freeze water, it **becomes ice**.
(condition)   (result)

If you're from Japan, you **must speak** Japanese.
(condition)   (assumption)

You **must be** tired **if** you have two jobs.
   (assumption)   (condition)

Without *must*, the sentence means that the speaker knows that what he or she is saying is true.

9 Work with a partner. Finish each sentence below as a factual conditional. Compare your ideas with the other pairs in your class.

1. If you are a good student, you _____.
2. If you work two jobs and go to night school, you _____
_____.
3. If you've never gotten a speeding ticket, you _____.
4. If you have been studying English for ten years, you _____
_____.

10 Work with a partner. Match the following clauses. Make up two sentences for each pair.

Example: *have two jobs   be very tired*
You must be very tired if you have two jobs.
OR If you have two jobs, you must be very tired.

A	B
1. are from Chicago	pay high taxes
2. live in Alaska	be a motivated student
3. are going to night school	be a Chicago Bulls fan
4. have many children	enjoy cold weather
5. are self-employed	get cavities
6. eat a lot of sugar	do a lot of cooking and laundry

Reflexive Pronouns/*Each other*

Bob and Sal are boxing. They are hitting **each other**.

(Bob is hitting Sal, and Sal is hitting Bob.)

> Reflexive pronouns:
> *myself, yourself,
> himself, herself,
> ourselves, yourselves,
> themselves.*

Sergio helps Gloria with her ESL homework.
Gloria helps Sergio with his tax forms.
Sergio and Gloria help **each other**.

Sergio hurt **himself** when he was fixing his car.

When one person does something to a second person and the second person does the same thing to the first person, you can use *each other*. You can use reflexive pronouns for what a person does to him- or herself.

11 Combine each pair of sentences into one sentence, using *each other*. Compare your answers with a classmate.

Example: *Sergio likes Gloria. Gloria likes Sergio.
Sergio and Gloria like each other.*

1. Yoshiko just met Amir's wife. Amir's wife just met Yoshiko.

2. Brazil hasn't played Mexico yet this season. Mexico hasn't played Brazil yet this season.

3. Jean respects her students. Jean's students respect her.

4. Gloria has written to her aunt many times. Gloria's aunt has written to her many times.

5. Thuy hasn't hit her brother all day. Her brother hasn't hit Thuy all day.

12 Now combine each pair of sentences. Use *each other* or *themselves*. Write the new sentences below.

Example: *Keiko hurt herself. Keiko's brother hurt himself.*
Keiko and her brother hurt themselves.

1. Tan cut himself while he was shaving. Amir cut himself while he was shaving.

   _____

2. Gloria treated herself to a hot fudge sundae. Helena treated herself to a hot fudge sundae.

   _____

3. Argentina has never played England in a championship soccer match. England has never played Argentina in a championship soccer match.

   _____

4. Sergio gave Gloria a birthday present. Gloria gave Sergio a birthday present.

   _____

Connections: Expressing Assumptions

You can use *must* to express assumptions. For example, you can say, "You must be exhausted" or "He must be very depressed" when you are 95% sure something is true.

Sergio's mother: Grace, guess what? Sergio got into the Art Institute of Chicago.
Grace: Oh, what fantastic news! You must be very proud of him.

Ana: Jean, what's the matter? You don't look very good.
Jean: Well, maybe it's because tonight's the last night of class.
Ana: Oh, you must be really sad. I know how you love the people in your class.
Jean: Yes, I'll really miss them.

Tan: Jean, I have really good news. I got a job at the Social Security Department.
Jean: Oh, great! You must be very pleased.

13 Work with a partner. Practice the conversation in Connections above. Then use the conversations as a model to make your own conversation. Share it with the class.

156   Unit 15

14 Work in a group. Share good news and bad news that group members have had recently. Role-play conversations about good news and bad news like the ones on page 156. Share your role-plays with the class.

15 Superstitions are beliefs that are not true. Below are some common superstitions in the U.S. Complete the sentences. Draw a line from the clause in Column 1 to a clause in Column 2. Compare your answers with a partner.

1	2
If your palm itches	you will have bad luck
If you see a shooting star	you're going to kiss a fool
If you walk under a ladder	your wish will come true
If you find a four-leaf clover	you'll get some money
If your nose itches	you'll have good luck

Are any of the superstitions above the same in your country? Which ones? Tell the class about other superstitions in your country.

Partnerwork ▶ Person A

Work with a partner. Person A looks at this page only. Person B looks at page 158 only.

Read the two sets of clauses below. They are about the people in this book. Match the clauses in the first set with the clauses in the second set. If you can't match the clauses on this page, ask your partner. He or she might have the matching clause. When you and your partner have matched as many clauses as you can, write sentences like this one: "If Sergio goes to the Art Institute, he will become a successful artist." Then share your sentences with the class.

1. If Victor gets a promotion   2. Sergio will become a successful artist   3. Helena will sing again   4. Chan Ho Cho will sell his restaurant   5. Amir will buy a new car   6. If Ana and Jean go to Arizona again   7. If Gloria quits her job as a waitress

1. If the Metropolitan Opera accepts her   2. She won't have any money   3. If Yoshiko goes back to Japan   4. He will start to save money to open a business   5. Ana will move to New York   6. If Sergio doesn't get a scholarship   7. Amir will drop his English classes

Partnerwork ▶ Person B

Work with a partner. Person B looks at this page only. Person A looks at page 157 only.

Read the two sets of clauses below. They are about the people in this book. Match the clauses in the first set with the clauses in the second set. If you can't match the clauses on this page, ask your partner. He or she might have the matching clause. When you and your partner have matched as many clauses as you can, write sentences like this one: "If Sergio goes to the Art Institute, he will become a successful artist." Then share your sentences with the class.

1. If someone gives him a good offer 2. If Tan gets a good job 3. They won't drive through the desert 4. If Helena quits her job at the factory 5. She'll have to find a job 6. If he gets a really good job 7. If her illustrations are successful

1. If he gets a raise 2. He won't move to Chicago 3. He won't have to patrol the street anymore 4. If he gets into the Art Institute 5. She will have plenty of free time 6. If he has to work too hard at his job 7. She'll have to start all over again

In Your Own Words

What are your plans for the future? Use *will* and *won't* to write three or four predictions about your future. Then read your predictions aloud and discuss your plans with a group.

Wrapping Up

Each person in the class will think of a conditional sentence about one of his or her classmates. Each sentence must have one *if* clause and one *will* clause. Write each clause on a separate piece of paper. First, your teacher will collect the *will* papers and pass them out. Then your teacher will do the same thing with the *if* papers. Walk around the class and try to put the clauses together to make logical sentences. Write your sentences on the board.

Example: *If Gloria doesn't stop eating hot fudge sundaes, she will have to buy bigger jeans.*

If Helena gets a part in the city opera, she will be the happiest woman in the world.

Review: Units 13–15

1. Work in small groups of six or eight. Divide each group into two teams. Team members make up six sentences about themselves and their classmates using *when* or *while* and the past continuous. Write each half of the sentence on a slip of paper. Teams exchange slips.

    Make a game board like the one below. Each box should be large enough for a piece of paper. Mix up the papers from one team. Place them face down on the game board. Members of the other team play the game first. Members take turns turning over two papers. If they make a logical sentence, the team gets one point. After each person's turn, place the two pieces of paper face down. After ten turns, switch teams.

    Example: *I was sleeping / when the telephone rang.*

1	2	3	4
5	6	7	8
9	10	11	12

2 One person is "it." That person quietly tells the teacher who or what in the room he or she is thinking about. Classmates then take turns asking ten yes/no questions to discover what "it" is thinking about. Make questions with *who*, *that*, or *which*.

Example: Student: I'm thinking of someone in the room.
Class: Are you thinking of someone who is tall?
Student: Yes, this person is tall.
Class: Are you thinking of someone that is from Asia?
Student: Yes.
Class: Are you thinking of someone who's single?
Student: No, this person is not single.
Class: Is the person that you're thinking of from Japan?
Student: Yes.
Class: Is it Yoshiko?
Student: Yes!

3 Divide the class into two teams of equal size. Each team writes a sentence for every member of the other team. Half of the sentences are situations in which a classmate wants to borrow something from someone. The other half are the promises that classmate will make to care for the borrowed item.

Teams then mix up their pieces of paper and pass them out to the other team members. Each student must memorize his or her sentence. All students walk around and say their sentences until they find the situation that matches their promise. When everyone has found his or her partner, form a line and share all the situations and promises.

Example: Situation: Chan Ho's son wants to borrow his father's car.
Promise: I'll put gas in it, and I won't speed.

Teacher Script for Listening Exercises

Unit 1

Page 2
Exercise 1
1. Takeshi walks to work every day.
2. Manuel lives in Texas.
3. Maria misses her friends in Colombia.
4. Will reads all the time.

Page 6
Exercise 9
1. Sergio runs three miles every day.
2. Look! Lisa's running down the street.
3. Chan Ho has two cups of coffee every morning.
4. Tan is washing his clothes. They'll be dry in an hour.
5. Yolanda smokes a pack of cigarettes a day.
6. Why is it so smoky in here? Ron's smoking a cigar.
7. Cas speaks two languages besides English.
8. Right now, Cas is speaking English with his ESL teacher.
9. Trung's reading the paper, but he'll have to leave in about five minutes.
10. Masha comes to class late every day.

Unit 2

Page 17
Exercise 13
1. I completed my training last year, so now I'm working as a dental assistant.
2. I used to be a factory worker, but I got married and left my job.
3. I used to have a terrible job. I hated it. Then I got a job as a real estate agent. I'm very happy with it.
4. Five years ago, I was a farm worker in California. Now I'm a truck driver.
5. Last year I started my job as a police officer. I love it.

Unit 3

Page 23
Exercise 4
1. started
2. lived
3. worked
4. driven
5. eaten
6. given
7. lasted
8. talked

Page 24
Exercise 7
1. Marla's out. She's gone to the dentist.
2. Ramón and I have done our homework.
3. Have you ever worked in a restaurant?
4. Rita's lived in L.A. all her life.

Unit 5

Page 44
Exercise 1
1. Could you please help me open this door?
2. Can you give me that book over there?
3. Will you get the phone, Jack?
4. Would you please talk to him for me?
5. Could you give me directions to the post office?

Unit 6

Page 54
Exercise 1
1. I'd like some ice cream right now.
2. I like to read. What about you?
3. I like wine with dinner.
4. I'd like to talk to you.
5. I'd like some coffee.
6. I like Chinese tea.

Unit 7

Page 66
Exercise 1
1. I'd like a small glass of water, please.
2. There's fruit on the table next to the rice.
3. Here's some advice for you: don't bet on the horses.
4. We need two teaspoons of oil, an onion, and salt and pepper.
5. The fog is so heavy today that I can't see the buildings across the street.
6. The snow hasn't melted yet.
7. Bring four chairs and four bowls of soup.

Page 69
Exercise 6
First heat the oil in a large frying pan. Add the mustard seeds. When the seeds start to pop, add the salt, curry powder, garlic, and onion. Cook and stir for 5 minutes. Add the eggplant. Cook and stir for 15 minutes. Serve immediately over rice.

Unit 8

Page 76
Exercise 1
1. Sergio gave a birthday card to Jean.
2. Amir bought a nice watch for his brother Salar in Iran.
3. Yoshiko bought a new sweater for Keiko.
4. Helena made a skirt for Jean.
5. Jean gave good grades to her class.

Page 79
Exercise 8
1. A: Tan, what did you buy your family?
   B: I bought them tickets to the U.S.
2. A: Amir, are you still looking for something for your brother?
   B: No. I found a really nice watch for him yesterday.
3. A: What are you doing, Yoshiko?
   B: I'm wrapping a present. I bought Keiko a new sweater.
4. A: Why is Chan Ho so tired?
   B: He made a special meal for Jean at his restaurant last night.

Unit 9

Page 89
Exercise 7
1. Amir, let's go to lunch sometime, what do you say?
2. Sergio, would you like to go to the movies tomorrow night with Jean and me?
3. Yoshiko, how'd you like to join us for lunch this afternoon?
4. Victor, let's go out for dinner sometime, OK?

Page 92
Exercise 14
1. With a cut like that, you better go to the doctor.
2. I can't talk right now. I gotta go.
3. Ramón can't come today. He hasta work late.
4. I hafta leave class early today.
5. What do I hafta do if I file my taxes late?
6. You gotta help me. My car's stuck in the snow.

Unit 10

Page 98
Exercise 1
1. Go straight until the red light.
2. When you see a gas station, you turn right.
3. You go down the street and you turn left at the corner.
4. You go straight until you see a big hotel.
5. Go past the fountain and turn left at the lion house.
6. You turn left at the light, and you'll see the store immediately.

Page 99
Exercise 2
First you turn left and go around the fountain until you come to the elephants. Then you turn left and go past the elephants until you come to the next walkway. Then you turn right at the walkway and go straight. You'll see the giraffes on the left.

Page 104
Exercise 11
1. When Victor went downtown, he ran into Chan Ho.
2. Yoshiko is looking for Japanese seaweed for dinner tonight.
3. Jean calls on Gloria a lot because she often knows the answers.
4. Amir looks like his father, who is very dark-haired and thin.
5. Jean was in Mexico for two weeks, and she came back last weekend.
6. Helena hasn't gotten over culture shock in the U.S., but she is trying to adapt.

Unit 11

Page 108
Exercise 1
1. Victor will be home tonight.
2. It might rain on Saturday.
3. Yoshiko should be here a bit later.
4. Wear your boots. There may be a lot of snow on the ground.

Page 109
Exercise 3
1. Scientists might find a cure for cancer in the next 30 years.
2. Your letter to Mexico should arrive by next week.
3. The trains will be on schedule tomorrow.
4. Malik may have problems with this lesson.

Unit 13

Page 130
Exercise 1
1. Two days ago, Amir was still waiting for a letter from his brother in Teheran.
2. At eight o'clock yesterday evening, Helena was listening to *Halka*, her favorite opera.
3. What were you doing at the time of the murder?
4. Victor was driving too fast.
5. Amir was washing the dishes, and Hushi was drying them.
6. Outside the classroom, Yoshiko was holding a present for Jean behind her back.

Unit 14

Page 145
Exercise 10
1. The *Daily Gazette* is a local newspaper that gives weather information from around the world.
2. Sergio is a friend of mine who is a really good artist.
3. Helena is looking for a job which will give her more free time.
4. Gloria has a job that doesn't pay very much.
5. Tan is the one who always does well on tests.

Page 147
Exercise 15
1. Oh, look outside. What a beautiful day!
2. They asked me why they should hire me. How bizarre!
3. For dessert they served me something green and transparent. What strange food!
4. Is that your new baby? What a cute child!
5. Are those your kids? What cute children!
6. Your aunt died? What terrible news!
7. There was an earthquake yesterday in India. How terrible!
8. This is Ron's new book. How interesting!
9. She wants to work as a beekeeper. What an idea!

Teacher Script

Appendix

Simple Past of *Be*

Statements

| I / He / She / It | **was** | home yesterday. |

| We / You / They | **were** | home yesterday. |

Negative Statements

| I / He / She / It | **wasn't** | home yesterday. |

| We / You / They | **weren't** | home yesterday. |

Questions

| **Was** | I / he / she / it | home yesterday? |

| **Were** | we / you / they | home yesterday? |

- Negative statements and questions in the simple past of *be* are formed without an auxiliary.

- Negative statements have *not* after the verb (contractions: *was not → wasn't, were not → weren't*).

- Questions are formed by inverting the subject and verb: *I was → Was I?* *Wh*-questions place a *wh*-question word before the verb.

Simple Past of Regular Verbs

Statements

I	**worked**	well.	He	**worked**	well.
We			She		
You			It		
They					

Negative Statements

I	**didn't work**	well.	He	**didn't work**	well.
We			She		
You			It		
They					

Questions

Did	I	**work** well?	**Did**	he	**work** well?
	we			she	
	you			it	
	they				

- Regular verbs form the past tense of statements by adding *-ed* to the verb (*work* → *worked*).

- Negative statements and questions in the simple past of verbs other than *be* are formed with the auxiliary *did* (the past-tense form of the verb *do*).

- Negative statements have *not* after the auxiliary (contractions: *did not* → *didn't*).

- Questions are formed by inverting *did* and the subject; the main verb comes after the subject: *You worked* → *Did you work? Wh*-questions place a *wh*-question word before *did*.

Appendix

Pronunciation of the Simple Past

When we say the simple past form of most verbs, we add a /t/ or a /d/ sound to them. We do not say an extra syllable when we say the past form. (When we write the simple past form, it always ends in -ed.)

Examples:

	/t/ sound	/d/ sound
	stop—stopped 1 1	rob—robbed 1 1
	look—looked 1 1	wave—waved 1 1
	watch—watched 1 1	play—played 1 1

We do add an extra syllable when the simple form of the verb ends in a *t* or *d* sound.

Examples:

	wait—waited 1 1 2	need—needed 1 1 2
	want—wanted 1 1 2	decide—decided 1 2 1 2 3

Simple Past (Irregular Verbs)

Here are some of the more common irregular verbs and their simple past forms.

Simple Form	Simple Past Form	Simple Form	Simple Past Form
be	was/were	let	let
become	became	lose	lost
begin	began	make	made
break	broke	mean	meant
bring	brought	meet	met
buy	bought	pay	paid
choose	chose	put	put
come	came	read	read
cost	cost	ride	rode
do	did	run	ran
draw	drew	say	said
drink	drank	see	saw
drive	drove	set	set
eat	ate	sing	sang
feel	felt	speak	spoke
find	found	spend	spent
forget	forgot	stand	stood
get	got	take	took
give	gave	teach	taught
go	went	tell	told
have	had	think	thought
hear	heard	understand	understood
hit	hit	wake	woke
keep	kept	wear	wore
know	knew	write	wrote
leave	left		

Past Participles (Irregular Verbs)

Here are some of the more common irregular verbs and their past participles. To form the present perfect, use **have** + the past participle of the main verb.

Simple Form	Past Participle	Simple Form	Past Participle
be	been	leave	left
become	become	let	let
begin	begun	lose	lost
break	broken	make	made
bring	brought	mean	meant
buy	bought	meet	met
choose	chosen	pay	paid
come	come	put	put
cost	cost	read	read
do	done	ride	ridden
draw	drawn	run	run
drink	drunk	say	said
drive	driven	see	seen
eat	eaten	set	set
feel	felt	sing	sung
find	found	speak	spoken
forget	forgotten	spend	spent
get	gotten	stand	stood
give	given	take	taken
go	gone	teach	taught
have	had	tell	told
hear	heard	think	thought
hit	hit	understand	understood
keep	kept	wear	worn
know	known	write	written

1 Write the past participle of these verbs.

1. be _____been_____
2. bring _____
3. do _____
4. drink _____
5. drive _____
6. forget _____
7. know _____
8. see _____
9. take _____
10. tell _____
11. think _____
12. write _____

Spelling of Plural Nouns

Spelling Rules	Examples
1. Add -s to most singular nouns.	fork—forks, boy—boys, price—prices, nose—noses
2. Add -es to nouns that end in these letters: s, z, sh, ch, and x.	glass—glasses, dish—dishes, inch—inches, box—boxes
3. When the simple form ends in -y after a consonant, change the y to i and add -es.	baby—babies, lady—ladies, party—parties, berry—berries
4. When the simple form ends in -o after a consonant, add -es.[1]	tomato—tomatoes, potato—potatoes
5. For nouns that end in -f or -fe, change the -f or -fe to -ves.[2]	leaf—leaves, knife—knives, shelf—shelves
6. There are also some irregular nouns. Here are some common ones.	person—**people**, man—**men**, woman—**women**, child—child**ren**, foot—**feet**, tooth—**teeth**, mouse—**mice**, goose—**geese**

1 Write the plural form of these nouns.

1. rose _____
2. table _____
3. toy _____
4. house _____
5. man _____
6. person _____
7. lady _____
8. knife _____
9. class _____
10. tomato _____
11. mouse _____
12. woman _____
13. child _____
14. strawberry _____

[1]There are some exceptions to this rule (e.g., piano—pianos).
[2]There are some exceptions to this rule (e.g., chief—chiefs).

Two-Word Verbs

Here are some common two-word verbs. There are many more two-word verbs in English. New ones are being created all the time as the need arises. Many two-word verbs have more than one meaning. You may wish to add more two-word verbs to this list as you learn them.

Verb	**Meaning**	**Example Sentence**
call back	(telephone again)	Can I call you back in five minutes?
call off	(cancel)	I called the party off because I was sick.
call up	(telephone)	I called her up yesterday.
check out	(borrow from a library or office)	He checked out three books from the library.
clean up	(clean completely)	They cleaned up the kitchen after dinner.
find out	(learn something)	How did you find out her age?
give back	(return)	I'll give your book back tomorrow.
give up	(stop doing something)	He gave up smoking two weeks ago.
look up	(search for something in a book)	I looked the word up in the dictionary.
pick up	(go and get a person or thing)	I'll pick you up at 7 o'clock.
put on	(wear)	Put on a coat. It's cold outside.
put away	(put in the place where something is kept)	She put her clothes away.
turn down	(decrease the volume) OR (refuse a job offer)	Please turn the radio down. It's too loud. I turned down the job because the pay was too low.

Appendix

turn off	(stop a machine)	Please turn off the TV.
turn on	(start a machine)	Please turn on the lights. It's dark in here.
turn up	(increase the volume)	Please turn the radio up. I can't hear it.
wake up	(make a person stop sleeping)	Please be quiet. You'll wake up the children.
write down	(make notes)	She wrote down the information.

Weights and Measures

Weight

Units: ounce, pound, ton

16 ounces (oz.) = 1 pound (lb.)
2,000 pounds = 1 ton (t.)

Liquid and Dry

Units: fluid ounce, cup, pint, quart, gallon, teaspoon, tablespoon

8 fluid ounces = 1 cup (c.)
2 cups (c.) = 1 pint (pt.)
2 pints = 1 quart (qt.)
4 quarts = 1 gallon (gal.)
3 teaspoons (tsp.) = 1 tablespoon (tbsp.)

Distance

Units: inch, foot, yard, mile

12 inches (in.) = 1 foot (ft.)
3 feet = 1 yard (yd.)
1,760 yards = 1 mile (mi.)

Comparative Adjectives

The following chart explains spelling rules and when to use *-er* or *more* with comparative adjectives.

Spelling Rules	Examples
One-Syllable Adjectives Add *-er* to one-syllable adjectives. (If the adjective already ends in *-e*, add only an *-r*.)	fast—faster cheap—cheaper large—larger
For one-syllable adjectives that end in a single vowel and a single consonant, double the consonant. Then add *-er*.	big—bigger thin—thinner slim—slimmer
Two-Syllable Adjectives For two-syllable adjectives that end in *-y*, change the *y* to *i* and add *-er*.	pretty—prettier ugly—uglier heavy—heavier
Other Adjectives with Two or More Syllables Use *more* with other adjectives that have two or more syllables.	useful—more useful beautiful—more beautiful dangerous—more dangerous expensive—more expensive
Irregular Adjectives These adjectives are irregular.	good—better bad—worse far—farther (distance)

1 Write the comparative form of each adjective.

1. fast _faster_
2. slow _____
3. big _____
4. thin _____
5. large _____
6. pretty _____
7. heavy _____
8. useful _____
9. beautiful _____
10. expensive _____
11. dangerous _____
12. good _____
13. bad _____
14. far _____

Appendix   173

Superlative Adjectives

The following chart explains spelling rules and when to use *-est* or *the most* with superlative adjectives.

Spelling Rules	Examples
One-Syllable Adjectives Add *-est* to one-syllable adjectives. (If the adjective already ends in *-e*, add only *-st*.)	fast—the fastest cheap—the cheapest large—the largest
For one-syllable adjectives that end in a single vowel and a single consonant, double the consonant. Then add *-est*.	big—the biggest thin—the thinnest slim—the slimmest
Two-Syllable Adjectives For two-syllable adjectives that end in *-y*, change the *y* to *i* and add *-est*.	pretty—the prettiest ugly—the ugliest heavy—the heaviest
Other Adjectives with Two or More Syllables Use *the most* with other adjectives that have two or more syllables.	useful—the most useful beautiful—the most beautiful dangerous—the most dangerous expensive—the most expensive
Irregular Adjectives These adjectives are irregular.	good—the best bad—the worst far—the farthest

1 Write the superlative form of each adjective.

1. fast _the fastest_
2. slow _____
3. big _____
4. thin _____
5. large _____
6. pretty _____
7. heavy _____
8. useful _____
9. beautiful _____
10. expensive _____
11. dangerous _____
12. good _____
13. bad _____
14. far _____

The United States

Appendix

World Map

Appendix

Answer Key

Unit 1
Page 2
Exercise 1
1. /s/
2. /z/
3. /iz/
4. /z/

Page 6
Exercise 9
1. runs
2. is running
3. has
4. is washing
5. smokes
6. is smoking
7. speaks
8. is speaking
9. is reading
10. comes

Page 7
Exercise 13
1. fixes . . . 's installing
2. owns . . . has
3. 's talking . . . greets
4. draws . . . 's drawing
5. reads . . . don't read
6. practice . . . know

Unit 2
Page 17
Exercise 13
1. She's a dental assistant.
2. She isn't a factory worker anymore.
3. He's a real estate agent.
4. He isn't a farm worker anymore.
5. She's a police officer.

Unit 3
Page 22
Exercise 2
1. invited, invited
2. visited, visited
3. watched, watched
4. studied, studied

Page 23
Exercise 3
1. done
2. had
3. gone
4. eaten
5. been

Exercise 4
1. started, 2
2. lived, 1
3. worked, 1
4. driven, 2
5. eaten, 2
6. given, 2
7. lasted, 2
8. talked, 1

Page 24
Exercise 7
1. has gone
2. have done
3. have worked
4. has lived

Unit 4
Page 36
Exercise 5
1. for
2. for
3. for
4. for
5. since
6. for
7. since

Page 39
Exercise 13
has had . . . was . . . was . . . decided . . .

have lived . . . has studied . . . has had . . . helped

Unit 5
Page 44
Exercise 1
1. formal request
2. informal request
3. informal request
4. formal request
5. formal request

178   Answer Key

Page 45
Exercise 2
1. Could you please help me open this door?
2. Can you give me that book over there?
3. Will you get the phone, Jack?
4. Would you please talk to him for me?
5. Could you give me directions to the post office?

Page 48
Focus on Vocabulary
1. clean up
2. plug in
3. take off
4. take out
5. hang up
6. put on

Page 50
Exercise 10
Request forms will vary.
1. Could you please take it out?
2. Could you throw it out?
3. Can you pick them up/Can you hang them up?

Unit 6
Page 54
Exercise 1
1. would like
2. like
3. like
4. would like
5. would like
6. like

Page 59
Exercise 9
1. one
2. another one
3. ones
4. one . . . one

Review: Units 4–6
Page 63
Exercise 3

Singular Nouns	Plural Forms
sister	sisters
job	jobs
store	stores
shoe	shoes
department	departments
clothing	—
dentist	dentists
tooth	teeth

Plural Nouns	Singular Forms
students	student
men	man
women	woman
children	child
stories	story
customers	customer
feet	foot
sneakers	sneaker
heels	heel
boots	boot
pairs	pair

Unit 7
Page 66
Exercise 1
1. a glass (count); water (noncount)
2. fruit (noncount); the table (count); the rice (noncount)
3. advice (noncount); the horses (count)
4. teaspoons (count); oil (noncount); an onion (count); salt (noncount); pepper (noncount)
5. the fog (noncount); the buildings (count); the street (count)
6. the snow (noncount)
7. chairs (count); bowls (count); soup (noncount)

Page 69
Exercise 6
From top to bottom, the directions should be numbered: 2, 4, 3, 6, 1, 7, 5

Unit 8
Page 76
Exercise 1

Direct Object	Indirect Object
1. birthday card	Jean
2. a nice watch	his brother Salar
3. a new sweater	Keiko
4. a skirt	Jean
5. good grades	her class

Page 77
Exercise 2

Direct Object	Indirect Object
1. candles	Jean
2. a card	the teacher
3. flowers	Jean

Here are the revised sentences:
1. They bought Jean candles.
2. Amir made the teacher a card.
3. Yoshiko gave Jean flowers.

Page 79
Exercise 8

Who	What	To or for which person
1. Tan	bought tickets to the U.S.	his family
2. Amir	found a really nice watch	his brother
3. Yoshiko	bought a new sweater	Keiko
4. Chan Ho	made a special meal	Jean

Answer Key 179

Exercise 9
1. for
2. for
3. to
4. for
5. to
6. to
7. to
8. for

Page 82
Exercise 12
1. Helena took her new dress back because it had a stain on it.
2. Yoshiko left the party early because she needed to pick up her children from the baby-sitter.
3. Gloria brought her camera to the party because she wanted to take some pictures.

Exercise 13
1. Victor's little brother got a lot of presents for Christmas, so he was very happy.
2. Sergio had to work the night of Jean's party, so he was upset.

Unit 9
Page 89
Exercise 7
1. general
2. specific
3. specific
4. general

Page 91
Exercise 12
1. has been studying
2. have been walking
3. have been watching
4. have been working
5. has been washing . . . has been drying
6. has been typing

Page 92
Exercise 14
1. With a cut like that, you'd better go to the doctor.
2. I can't talk right now. I've got to go.
3. Ramón can't come today. He has to work late.
4. I have to leave class early today.
5. What do I have to do if I file my taxes late?
6. You've got to help me. My car's stuck in the snow.

Unit 10
Page 98
Exercise 1

	With *You*	Without *You*
1.	—	go straight
2.	you turn	—
3.	you go . . . you turn	—
4.	you go	—
5.	—	go past . . . turn left
6.	you turn	—

Page 100
Exercise 5
through . . . toward . . . by . . . past

Page 102
Exercise 8
1. Sporting Goods
2. Health and Beauty
3. Shoes and Hosiery
4. Accessories or Jewelry
5. Housewares
6. Bath and Bedding
7. Hardware
8. Automotive
9. Shoes and Hosiery
10. Electronics
11. Appliances

Page 104
Exercise 11
1. ran into
2. is looking for
3. calls on
4. looks like
5. came back
6. hasn't gotten over

Page 105
Exercise 15
1. looks like
2. run into
3. get over
4. calls on

Unit 11

Page 108
Exercise 1
1. Certainly
2. Possibly
3. Probably
4. Quite possibly

Page 109
Exercise 2
Answers will vary.
1. It should rain in Seattle later today.
2. It might snow in Minneapolis tonight.
3. There might be a hurricane off the coast of Florida this weekend.
4. The sky will be clear and sunny in Tucson today.
5. There may be a tornado in the Midwest later in the week.

Page 109
Exercise 3
1. Scientists might find a cure for cancer in the next 30 years. 30% sure.
2. Your letter to Mexico should arrive by next week. 75% sure.
3. The trains will be on schedule tomorrow. 100% sure.
4. Malik may have problems with this lesson. 60% sure.

Page 111
Exercise 6
1. himself
2. myself
3. herself
4. themselves
5. himself . . . herself
6. ourselves

Page 112
Exercise 7
1. by herself
2. helped themselves
3. enjoyed herself
4. by herself
5. helped himself

Page 114
Exercise 10
1. fastest
2. longest
3. heaviest
4. most expensive
5. most poisonous
6. highest
7. most
8. worst

Unit 12

Page 122
Exercise 10
Answers will vary.
1. not as . . . as
2. not as . . . as, almost as . . . as
3. as . . . as
4. as . . . as

Page 123
Exercise 13
1. Cookies are more fattening than crackers.
2. Chicago is colder in the winter than New Orleans.
3. Tokyo is bigger than New York.
4. The population of China is bigger than the population of India.

Page 124
Focus on Vocabulary
1. mouse
2. feather
3. bear
4. rock
5. mule
6. bird

Unit 13

Page 130
Exercise 1
1. was waiting
2. was listening
3. were doing
4. was driving
5. was washing . . . was drying
6. was holding

Page 134
Exercise 8
1. Chou was cleaning the bathroom when she fell.
2. Alla was serving lunch when she spilled the soup.

Page 135
Exercise 9
Answers will vary.
1. Jean was driving when the car got a flat tire.
2. The hotel employees were talking and changing clothes when Gloria walked in.
3. Jean was having a cup of coffee when Ana arrived.

Page 137
Exercise 13
1. was waiting . . . started
2. was standing . . . sang
3. drew . . . was eating

Answer Key

Unit 14

Page 143
Exercise 5
1. day-care worker . . . who watches
2. dentist . . . who fills
3. reporter . . . who interviews
4. illustrator . . . who draws
5. construction worker . . . who builds

Page 145
Exercise 10
1. that which
2. who that
3. which that
4. that which
5. who that

Page 147
Exercise 15
1. a
2. no article
3. no article
4. a
5. no article
6. no article
7. no article
8. no article
9. an

Unit 15

Page 155
Exercise 11
1. Amir's wife and Yoshiko just met each other.
2. Brazil and Mexico haven't played each other yet this season.
3. Jean and her students respect each other.
4. Gloria and her aunt have written to each other many times.
5. Thuy and her brother haven't hit each other all day.

Page 156
Exercise 12
1. Tan and Amir cut themselves while they were shaving.
2. Gloria and Helena treated themselves to hot fudge sundaes.
3. Argentina and England have never played each other in a championship soccer match.
4. Sergio and Gloria gave each other birthday presents.